D1536481

Mr. Dickey

Secretary to Mary Baker Eddy

With A Chestnut Hill Album

Nancy Niblack Baxter

Hawthorne Publishing
Carmel, Indiana

Visit our website: www.hawthornepub.com
to see more interesting books.

Winds of Change Division
Hawthorne Publishing
15601 Oak Road Carmel, IN 46033
317-867-5183

Dedication

To the young girl who stood in 1920 in the back of her family's parlor and heard about a wonderful new book, Science and Health with Key to the Scriptures, Jane Fargo Baxter. For eight decades she has understood the Truth better than all others I know.

Contents

A Chestnut Hill Album

Foreword from the First Edition

I had only vague knowledge of Adam H. Dickey when I first became interested in Christian Science through his article, "God's Law of Adjustment." I later learned that he had been personal secretary to the religion's founder during the last years of Mary Baker Eddy's life and that she had depended on him. I also learned that he had helped lead her church at a crucial time immediately following her death in 1910. I did not know until much later that he had written a book.

The heirs to Dickey's memorabilia and papers, whom I have known all my adult life in Indianapolis, interested me in his life as well as in his other writings. The Dickey family had traveled the American path to success in the late 19th century, a path that led them both up and down. Although this book primarily explores the career of "Mr. Dickey," as he was usually called by Christian Scientists, the detailing here of the lives of family members in the business world beyond Boston serves as a counter theme to his devotion to a spiritual cause.

We are in a period in Christian Science history when analysis and reflection are needed. Biographies of Mary Baker Eddy have helped readers understand her as both a religious leader and a significant woman in 19th- and early 20th-century American society. Understanding the lives of some of the pioneers of Christian Science, who worked alongside Mrs. Eddy, can throw light on the Christian Science Church's past—as well as present and perhaps future. Through them we see the strength of inspired individual contributions and of the spiritual ideals that made their church the fastest growing denomination in America at the beginning of the last century.

I support gender-free identification for name titles; however, I have often retained "Mrs." and "Mr." when they seemed appropriate. Not only do these gentler forms sound proper to the ear, but also they reflect usage during the Victorian and Edwardian ages.

Nancy Niblack Baxter

Acknowledgments

This book would not have been possible without the help of two men. Keith "Skip" McNeil's extraordinary collection of Christian Science materials, acquired over some thirty years, provided many necessary documents, but beyond that, Skip filled in gray or difficult areas of church history directly for me. Denis Glover, formerly lifestyle editor of *The Christian Science Monitor* was the competent editor of the book and added his own insights from years in the movement.

I owe a debt of gratitude to others, also. Judy Huenneke and her capable staff at the Mary Baker Eddy Library for the Betterment of Humanity were good hosts at the library and made themselves available by both phone and e-mail. Personal researcher Deborah Scheetz stood in my stead, further seeking out materials. Cheryl Moneyhun at the Longyear Museum furnished valuable information from that archive.

Particular thanks go to Nancie Callender Baxter, whose name is like mine but who is a cousin, for encouragement and use of her Dickey family collection. And, to all the others who assisted in this quest, I say a heartfelt, "Thank you."

Chapter One

Roots in Protestant Soil

It is legendary that special times call forth special heroes—individuals unusually tempered by those times to meet the demands of the moment, often coming out of nowhere to save the day. For the Christian Science movement after the turn of the last century, at a time when the young denomination might have died, Adam Dickey was a modest hero fit for the moment. He was one of several, but his story is unique.

Dickey came to serve as his leader Mary Baker Eddy's personal secretary at her request three years before her 1910 passing and became a reliable aide in a difficult period. He helped the church transition in a time of change when many believed it could not endure—the passing of the woman whose inspiration and vitality had given the world a new religion based on Christian healing. Dickey served as the church's Treasurer, and in the period 1917-1921 he became a prominent representative of the board of directors, helping see the church through when factions threatened to split it apart.

So the legend holds true for the denomination that was the fastest growing religious phenomenon in American history. Every institution may have its person of the moment—Rome, its great Cincinnatus; the Revolution, its simple Molly Pitcher. Like Cincinnatus, Dickey was a truthful and dedicated "citizen soldier," raised from the ranks, willing to live in the rarified world first of the household of a famous religious leader and then in the intense atmosphere of administrative church politics. He was not without fault. Critics accused him of acting in contradictory ways, of letting power go to his head at times. Still, he sincerely served the cause he was devoted to, a simple man who did his duty but may often have just wanted to go home.

Adam Dickey did not exactly come from nowhere. His background and that of his family had been preparing him for years to understand the contentious battlefields of the soul in which were fought the struggle to help Christian Science endure.

Born in Toronto on June 26, 1864,[1] he was the son of Nathaniel and

Elizabeth Simpson Dickey. Nathaniel was an immigrant whose family had come from Ireland. Of most pride to this devotedly religious father were the Protestant credentials he brought with him.

The Dickeys had been drawn to spiritual pioneering. In the eighteenth century, Nathaniel's grandfather, also named Nathaniel, had accompanied John Wesley when he preached in Ireland. A journal written by the later Nathaniel describes his grandfather's hosting Wesley in his home and becoming a follower, converting from the Presbyterianism universally practiced in the Protestant north of Ireland. The revolutionary version of Christianity that was eighteenth-century Methodism became the Dickeys' church of choice.

In the narrative Nathaniel writes:

> In those days Presbyterians and Society of Friends were amongst the most sincere of the Christian Bodies, but the Church of England, as it was called, or the church by law established, was the only one that had its places of worship in nearly every part of the country, and they were the only ones in which the Early Methodists could go to have their children baptized, married or partake of the Sacrament. . . .Many of the lives of [the ministers of the established church] did not present any proper example of the followers of Christ.
>
> So destitute was the country of Evangelical services, that I remember hearing my father tell that upon one occasion, about one or two o'clock in the morning, he heard a loud knocking at his father's door and going to the window and asking who was there, a man answered by asking if that was where Nathaniel Dickey lived, and proceeded to state that he had come forty miles, riding one horse and leading another, to get my grandfather to go and pray with a man who was said to be dying.

In the eighteenth century Nathaniel Dickey became so active in Methodist gospel work, riding all over the territory near Londonderry, that his activities were suspected of having political overtones; this was the age of bitter fighting over Ireland. A magistrate examined him to see if he had connections to the feared invasion from France to wrench Ireland from England.

All of that Nathaniel's children were born in Ireland, including Adam Dickey's grandfather Adam (July 31, 1791), and the Methodist pioneer Nathaniel and his wife were buried in Magheragell near Drumshill in northern Ireland.

The grandson Nathaniel goes on in his narrative:

At different times all the . . .children came to America. [including Nathaniel's own father Adam Dickey] . . .All my father's brothers, with the exception of my Father . . .were men of large frame, handsome features, sandy complexion, and very strong constitutions.

Those active in managing The Christian Science Mother Church subsequently described the later Adam Dickey the same way.

Nathaniel Dickey, the father of our Adam, tells in the family history the story of his sailing from Ireland to new opportunities on the American continent.

In 1849, I, accompanied by my brother James and Miss Agnes and Miss Jane Neill (sisters of John Neill, my brother-in-law) sailed from Belfast in August in a small sailing vessel named "Standard." We were eight weeks on the water. Landed at Montreal; and there took Steamer "Princess" for Toronto.

In Canada Nathaniel took a job in a machine-shop and eventually came to own it. Attending the local Methodist church, he accepted the commitment to Christ very seriously. A "covenant" written by Nathaniel shows how the young man believed a life ought to be lived. It became a favorite document with Adam, his own son.

August 7, 1859

In the name of the Father and of the Son and of the Holy Ghost. I thus solemnly enter into a covenant with my Creator and Redeemer, having for its end the Glory of God and the Salvation of my soul.

And that I may be direct aright at this time, I Beseech Thee, Heavenly Father to grant me the enlightening influences of Thy Holy Spirit. Both to dictate the course most proper to be pursued and to strengthen me that I may be kept faithful in this discharge of the following duties, for Jesus' sake. Amen.

1st I give myselfe body soul and spirit into the hands of my Creator to be used as God's will may direct. 2nd That I will at least twice a day approach him in prayer for the pardon of my sins and full developement of my Christian character. 3rd That I will at least once each day read and try to understand some portion of his holy word. 4th That I will endeavor to become reconciled to any whome I may be at variance and make retribution to such as I may have in any way injured. 5th That in all matters of doubt

and uncertainty I will keep the example of Jesus before me &
endeavor to act according to my knowledge of His will.

But all was not piety and prayer. A note stuck into his journal, written
in 1859, shows that a pretty young woman had caught his eye. He courted
her, but apparently it was not going well, possibly because his intended
believed their age difference meant trouble—he was many years older. He
wrote to Elizabeth Simpson, daughter of the mayor of Barrie, a town near
Toronto.

> By people that are very wise I've often heard it said
> If ladies have a cat or dog, they're sure to die a maid
> Though fate may sometimes make it so,
> I hope this time 'twill miss it
> Though you more than love the pup,
> you even hug and kiss it.
> But ah! It surely cannot be that one so fair and good
> Should think of living all their life in single solitude
> But if the fates will have it so, I'll never cease to fret!!!
> Or even, if you kiss it much, to wish I were your CAT
> Barrie, Dec 5th, 1859
> ND

Nathaniel married Elizabeth on November 1, 1860, in Toronto. Their
first son was Walter Simpson, born June 26, 1862, and then Adam Herbert
two years later on the same day.

Elizabeth Simpson Dickey always proudly described her independent
Protestant heritage, too, writing numerous genealogical tracts and summa-
ries for her own children which survive in the family collection. Her Quaker
ancestors, John and Grace Holingshead, emigrated to Pennsylvania in the
1660s, leaving two children buried in the Chequer Alley cemetery, where
Quaker leaders John Bunyan and George Fox had also been laid to rest. The
Holingsheads remained active Quakers in the colony and intermarried with
other Protestants who became Elizabeth's ancestors.

The Dickeys lived in Toronto for twenty-five years, raising nine children. Nathaniel involved himself in the local politics and ran as a Liberal
Party candidate for Parliament in 1870. His opponent was a member of
Parliament who had been unseated because of bribery and ran again for
his seat. In a later account for a Kansas City newspaper,[2] Dickey contended
he would have been elected if it had not been for a snowfall that prevented
him from final campaigning and hindered the turnout. He lost by only a
few votes.

Meanwhile his machine-shop business, run in partnership with his
brother and brother-in-law, prospered. But the family fortunes were not to
be in Canada; they lay farther south.

Chapter Two

Up-to-date Kansas City

The Panic of 1873 brought the booming North American economy to a halt, and everything changed for the Dickeys. Nathaniel Dickey found himself trying to avoid bankruptcy and salvage a part of what had been something of a fortune.

According to a book by his grandson, Kenneth McMullen Dickey, Nathaniel had been:

> a proprietor of a large machine shop, with a political bent that made him City councilman for 20 years and a religious leaning that took much of his time as a Methodist layman. He could not keep the three balls of activity in the air. He dropped his bread and butter one, the machine shop, and went busted in the "Panic of '73."[1]

Nathaniel struggled for a few years to regain the ground that had been lost. But he had a wife and growing children to think of. By the early 1880s Walter, the oldest, was out of school and working, a young dandy who enjoyed biking around the town and developing astute business experience as an accountant in a wholesale jewelry firm. Adam, the second son, was graduating from the Model School, one of several institutions set up in the late nineteenth century to become showcases for the best educational trends.

In 1880 Nathaniel had traveled to Kansas City, Missouri, on a "pleasure trip," but probably with some personal economic motives, also. Thirty years later he told the Methodist newspaper *Central Christian Advocate* that the place captivated him. There might be a future in this bustling cow town, but Nathaniel Dickey was at first unwilling to subject his upright family to the "wickedness apparent" there. But the "wickedness" either abated or Nathaniel learned to live with it and found a way to protect his family.

The Dickeys were to move their family headquarter to become builders of society and industry in a Kansas City on the rise. Originally established by Rene Chouteau as an Indian-French trading post, it had grown substantially from its founding days. A few leading families, capitalizing on river trade and the beginnings of a cattle market, turned it from a crude frontier settlement of wooden dwellings, bars, and houses of ill fame into a city of brick homes, a thriving newspaper, and churches—a city destined for economic growth by 1860. It boomed during the Civil War period, when it weathered the many changes of fortune of a Missouri torn between Union supporters and Confederate raiders. Although never quite shedding its reputation as a town of sinners, by the time Dickey arrived Kansas City was experiencing the same industrial growth of many other American cities in the period 1880-1890.

Nathaniel rented an office and listed himself in the City Directory as "capitalist." He was seeking an investment that would help him recoup his lost prosperity and take care of his growing brood. By this time son Adam was pursuing studies at Upper Canada College, but his father would soon need his talents in Kansas City. First, though, Nathaniel had to get established.

Kenneth McM. Dickey writes in *A Man With Clay Feet*:

> W.H. Craig, a real estate speculator in the then growing town, went to N. Dickey and proposed that he take $5,000 in stock of the Kansas City Sewer Pipe Co—a new concern which Craig was organizing with a capital stock of $50,000. N. Dickey agreed and ground was broken for the 4-kiln plant, in the East Bottoms, adjoining the Missouri Pacific roundhouse. The business was not a failure nor very successful, account of bad management—as N. Dickey saw it. But he could do little about it as he was a minority stockholder, had other interests and the ever present urge to grind out tracts respecting the spiritual emoluments of Methodism.

In 1885 Nathaniel wrote Walter, telling his son he needed him to protect his interests in the Kansas City Sewer Pipe Company. With the approval of W. H. Craig, the senior partner, he offered Walter the job of general manager. Walter hurried south, leaving behind his fiancé, Katherine Letitia McMullen, the socially prominent daughter of a member of Parliament. But he would soon return to marry her and move her to Missouri.

Adam Dickey followed and joined the clay pipe business with his father and brother. He was given the position of "traveling salesman," an assignment that took note of Adam's ability with people; his brother presumably had other skills. The whole family was settled there by 1886.

Walter began to apply management techniques to the running of the company, and it took on new life. Adam for his part traveled to many sections of the country to promote the idea of sanitary sewers, a new cause in the nation.

America was in the midst of a modern city services revolution that had begun about 1875. Electric lights began to appear in major cities in the late 1870s. By the turn of the century, telephone party lines were even coming to country roads outside towns, and in the 1880s, when the Dickeys took up the clay pipe business, the movement to improve waste treatment was well underway.

Public ill health had for some time been attributed to the use of communal water sources, rivers, and streams that ran foul in the summer, especially contaminated wells and open sewers in trenches along the road. The "good water" movement would reach its height about 1910-1915, but it was changing opinions and practice as early as the 1880s. Funded debt and bond issues made it possible for municipalities to meet the demand for improved water systems and sewerage. Groups of local citizens or the municipalities themselves set up public service companies, selling stock to organize water retention and distribution services for large and eventually not-so-large populations.

Clearly the opportunity was there not only for making money but also for serving the public. The earliest pipe systems, put in before the Civil War, carried away both waste water and storm water. When there was an overflow, raw sewage flowed freely into streets and residential areas. A key event in Missouri occurred in 1884 when Octave Chanute, the engineer largely responsible for building the bridge at Hannibal, began a campaign to inform the public about the necessity of separating storm water from waste.[2]

Technology had to keep pace with the need for better services. The process for producing good sewer pipe had been significantly improved with the introduction of vitrified clay pipe, and the social pressure for better waste water treatment accelerated the need for even more technological growth. Towns began to realize "modern" utilities, public water systems, would be marks of civic pride.

Indoor bathrooms with functioning water closets contributed to the need for pipes to carry waste from the bathroom to the river, or as the public facility movements improved, a treatment facility. Vitrified pipe, fired in a kiln, provided lasting strength and permanence. The vitrified pipe sanitary sewer system of the Statue of Liberty was installed by a rival company during the period Dickey Clay Pipe Company began business. During renovations to the Statue at the end of the twentieth century, it was discovered that its sewer system was still in good shape, more than a hundred years old.

Nathaniel Dickey was a minority stockholder in Kansas City Sewer Pipe, and Walter saw that holdings expansion was a key to the family's future success. There was trouble with Craig, the original owner, at this time anyway. He objected to some of the strategies Walter was envisioning, and he was also not happy with Adam and their brother Alfred Dickey's involvement.

So it was time to move beyond the Craig enterprise. About 1890 Walter Dickey went to Deepwater, Missouri, and offered to buy a faltering clay pipe business run by John and Will Perry—the Keith and Perry Coal Company. Without investment money and with the strong intention not to involve the family in any further stock holdings, Walter consummated the deal. He evidently purchased the plant on time payments, which he met promptly. Alfred became plant manager; Adam expanded his traveling sales calls.

The company was a sole proprietorship without stock, a fact that would impact the financial status of Adam Dickey in years to come because he had to live on salary and commission. Walter's son records that his father promised he would "share a melon" with Alfred and Adam, a promise never fulfilled.

Walter named his company "W. S. Dickey Clay Manufacturing Company" and soon acquired another plant in Kansas City. In the next few years the parent company would become the largest clay pipe manufacturer in the nation. Walter's strategy was not only to operate plants at full capacity, but also to acquire new operations. He did not usually build new plants. Instead, he undercut his competitors, then purchased their plants when they failed. He took pride in implementing what might be called "hostile takeovers" quickly, with the skill of a master swordsman. He bought a plant in Pittsburg, Kansas, then quickly acquired others in Texarkana and San Antonio, Texas; Birmingham, Alabama; and three plants in Chattanooga, Tennessee.

Adam Dickey often traveled for his brother, learning train schedules in the complicated network that was then railroading America, and perhaps having to answer questions about his brother's high-powered tactics.

Cutting out competitors by any means was only one of several robber-baron strategies that enabled Walter Dickey to earn the grudging respect of other "get-it-all-no-matter-what" businessmen of the time. Another gimmick described by Walter's son was his profiting on the means of distribution—the freight rate or "differential." Since Kansas City was an intermediate shipping point for many clay pipe orders, because they were being sent on either farther west or east—the company had a lower price of shipment per ton than similar companies. The differential freight price could be used to take jobs below competitors'costs. By 1905 the company president was profiting from the differential by about half-a-million dollars a year.

Walter also manipulated prices for the product and shipping costs by price-fixing with competitors. That this was illegal did not seem to trouble him or many others of that generation, who believed they were building America as well as their own personal fortunes by using rampant free enterprise. The Sherman Anti Trust Bill and the determination of Theodore

Roosevelt acted to restrain men like Walter, but not before they had earned huge fortunes and the often unmerited respect of their wealthy neighbors in Kansas City, where the Dickey family joined clubs, sponsored elaborate dinners, and built huge homes.

Today the Walter Dickey home there is a jaded tribute to the power of Midwestern robber barons. The residence now houses offices of the Arts and Sciences faculty of the University of Missouri, K. C. A five-story mansion built of structural steel on acres of rolling ground at 1500 Rockhill Road, it cost three-quarters-of-a-million dollars to build in 1912. Its walls were faced with hand-cut stone. It was the talk of the city. But that is ahead of the story.

Adam Dickey found himself troubled by his brother's questionable tactics and by the fact that he shared little with the hard-working brothers assisting him. By 1887 Adam had married a Kansas City girl, Lillian M. Selden. Their son, Herbert Clayton Dickey, was born October 24, 1888, but lived only until 1895. They never had other children.

Younger brother Fred came into the business at this time; his more passive nature seemed better attuned to the needs of working with a difficult brother.

But Walter Dickey and Adam were opposite sides of a coin. Walter became devoted to the take-all ethics of a boom generation; Adam eventually committed himself to the quieter ethics of a new Christian way of life. Both schools of thought became parts of an adolescent America emerging into its own as a leader of nations.

Walter had by this time consummated a deal that drew upon him the wrath of his brothers and sisters. He had convinced his father, who seemed to dote on this eldest child, to sign over his minority interest in the original Kansas City plant. Soon W. S. purchased the rest of the Craig stock, and the company was his. Some in Kansas City commented on Walter Dickey's avarice and his ostentation. How could a father so steeped in the Christian gospel not realize the moral pit his older son was slipping into? Others in the family wondered.

Did Nathaniel recognize the strength of Christian character the second son, Adam, still in the shadow of his older brother, was developing? Surely he did. In a letter to Adam Dickey written in 1910, Nathaniel speaks first of his wife's health and then goes on to discuss his sons' characters:

> The injury which caused her long confinement to bed has furnished opportunity for many conversations about the vicissitudes of our early family life, when all its members were at home and the usual number at the table was ten to twelve. Sometimes we would speak of the different temperaments and idiosyncrasies of each one of the family. Naturally in early life your mother

and I made large drafts on the future good time coming when all would be wings and no weights. None but those who have experienced it can tell the pleasures of parental anticipation or the dreamy speculations of the future. Of course the propensities of youth point more or less clearly to the character of the man. Your eldest brother, early in life, foreshadowed the traits of character which have distinguished him as accumulator of this world's goods. The things that other children usually destroy or throw away, he preserved and kept with secretive care till he was a man. Whether this be a virtue or a fault in character depends upon the use that is made of it. He seemed to possess by intuition the Jewish idea as to the right of the first born.

Your early inclinations were entirely different and characterized by no particular care for such things. Your character was an open book, having nothing of the secretive or mysterious in you. Indeed your frankness may be said to have amounted to indiscretion, and whether prompted by a love of the right or the natural pugnacity of your Irish temperament, one thing was clear—you were always ready to defend both by your voice and gesture whatever you thought was right or true.

Early in life you seemed gifted with an unusual fluency of speech and a marked tendency towards indulgence in recitation and discussion, always defending your opinions with an earnestness which amounted to obstinacy no doubt believing—as you once said to me later, that "whatever was right ought to be true and whatever was true ought to be defended." I well remember when a lad of 14 year or so of age you were appointed to take part in a debate of the question "Whether War or Intemperance has destroyed the greater number of Mankind." After the collection of statistics and some home coaching you chose the side of Intemperance and defended your position so earnestly and with such an array of fact and figures as to astonish the audience, and being hard pressed by your opponent you raised your voice and speaking with great vehemence and striking the desk with your fist exclaimed, "I know I am right, and I can prove it." Of course such a display of youthful energy brought down the house . . .

Like most boys, you sometimes required correction and reproof, but indeed boys who can be reared without such restraints do not seem to be worth much to me. I think it may be said that one of your greatest blessings is the gift of that vigilant keeper of the storehouse of knowledge, a good memory, the faculty, which above all others, is so often called upon to play the double part of both servant and master.

It is a pleasing thought to be able to say that in common with all our children you were reared in a Christian household, and were early taught the sacredness and importance of religion and respect for the Christian Sabbath, together with the manliness of truth and honesty of character in all things. . . .

The qualities observed by his father in Adam Dickey as a boy would be invaluable in the job he took up in the fourth decade of his life.

Adam Dickey at seventeen.
Courtesy Longyear Museum Collection

The Dickey family home in Toronto, built by Adam's father in the late 1860s. A cousin, Josie Dickey, stands in front.

Courtesy Elizabeth Dickey Herman Collection

> August 7th 1859
>
> In the Name of the Father & of the Son & of the Holy Ghost I thus Solemnly enter into a covenant with My Creator & Redeemer, having for its end the Glory of God & the Salvation of My soul.
>
> And that I may be directed aright at this time, I Beseech The Heavenly Father to grant Me the enlightening influences of thy Holy Spirit, Both to dictate the course Most proper to be persued & to strengthen Me that I may be kept faithfull in the discharge of the following duties, for Jesus Sake, Amen—
>
> 1st I give Myself Body Soul & spirit into the hands of My Creator to be used as Gods will may direct
>
> 2d That I will at least twice every day approach him in prayer for the pardon of My Sins & full development of My Christian character,
>
> 3d That I will at least once each day read & endeavour to understand Some portion of his holy word,
>
> 4th That I will endeavour to become reconciled to any with whome I may be at variance and Make restitution to such as I may have in anyway injured ———
>
> 5th That in all Matters of doubt or uncertainty I will keep the example of Jesus before Me & endeavour to act according to My knowledge of his will

Nathaniel Dickey's Covenant

Elizabeth Simpson Dickey, wife of Nathaniel and mother of Adam.
Courtesy Elizabeth Dickey Herman Collection

Fred Dickey as a youth. Adam's brother remained in the family business after Adam left.
Courtesy Elizabeth Dickey Herman Collection

The Dickey Family—1904: (standing) Louise, Alfred, Lillian (Lilla) Adam, Florence Margaret, Nathaniel ("Nat'). (seated) Fred Lionel, Harry, Mother Elizabeth Simpson, Father Nathaniel, Walter Simpson.
Courtesy Elizabeth Dickey Herman Collection

Chapter Three

Mr. Dickey Finds Christian Science

The Methodists in Nathaniel's Independence Avenue Methodist church, the members of Fred Dickey's hunt club in suburban Kansas City, and the executives at the W. L. Dickey clay pipe factories often talked about items they read about in the newspapers. They discussed the rather pompous presidency of Benjamin Harrison, séances the spiritualists were holding, the beginning enforcement of the Sherman Anti-trust law designed to curb monopolies like Standard Oil (and the Dickey clay companies) and all the fuss about "new women."

One of these women was particularly in the news. Groups talked with interest about her, because it allowed them to introduce into the discussions another popular topic: religion. Mary Baker Eddy's interpretation of Christianity was crossing the nation and gathering thousands of adherents. Nothing like it had been seen before, not even when the Mormons moved across the stage on their way to Utah forty years before. A new religion had been founded by this New Hampshire native, who lived and lectured now in Massachusetts.

Christian Science had come to Kansas City in the late 1880s. Services were listed in the August, 1890, *Christian Science Journal* at two separate halls.[1] Lecturers went about the country speaking about it, and many went to hear and spread the news, as did periodicals of the day. Some comments were not flattering; often they were just curious or informative. The followers of Mary Baker Eddy believed that primitive Christianity could be practiced now, on this earth, right in Kansas City. The sick could be healed and sin controlled through the understanding that the God of Love is all and the material world ultimately a delusion. Evil, disease, and death were nothing in eternal terms.

One could think the new religion might have merit and value it as an addition to the many kinds of Christianity being practiced in America at that time. Or one could be part of the school of skeptics, whose extreme proponents said it was complete sacrilege. Or one could believe Christian

Science was the truth.

Some well known Kansas City converts could tell you that knowing that God ruled as divine Spirit and no other power had a claim on mankind brought a practical form of salvation. It healed bodies, minds, and spirits. They said Jesus taught the method of divine healing through total reliance on God, but many in the modern churches were neglecting it. Christian Scientists and their neighbors told of people, some in their own families, who had been cured of years of lung trouble, influenza, dyspepsia , marriage failure, the demon rum. They were testifying in their church services to being healed of tuberculosis, measles, diphtheria, too.

Adam Dickey's wife Lillian and his sister Florence were intrigued, went to services in the Gibraltar Building, and soon were reading Mary Baker Eddy's book *Science and Health with Key to the Scriptures.*

The rest of the family retained a healthy skepticism. Methodism or the Disciples of Christ were good enough for them. Besides, there were no church suppers or ladies' guilds in "Science." The church was just for worship, spiritual learning, and testimony meetings where the power of prayer was glorified by those who had felt its touch. However, the rest of the family reasoned, it was well to be tolerant and allow new Protestant sects, particularly with so many Catholics in Kansas City. So sister Florence and Adam's wife Lillian began to go to both Sunday services and Wednesday evening meetings and learned to practice Christian Science, and the rest of the family showed whatever interest they could muster.

Lillian about this time experienced a serious physical problem which she later described as sciatica. Medical science could not heal it. She was restored to health through Christian Science.[2] A practitioner in the city, Henrietta E. Graybill, announced that she was holding a class in Christian Science practice. Mary Baker Eddy in Boston had offered her own classes and graduated a number of others to teach the religion. Mrs. Graybill of Kansas City was one of them.

Adam asked to accompany his wife to some of the classes. He soon saw that Christian Science promised to be a vision of what the Christian church he had loved so long might attain. This was an age of science, Mrs. Graybill said, and the church of Jesus needed to be scientific—to be able to prove all its claims. It had healed the sick and raised the dead in the first century; why couldn't that be part of Christian practice today?

The class must have answered Adam Dickey's questions about the woman who was teaching about these matters in Boston, who had written a book about them. Having been healed herself through prayer in 1866 of the results of serious fall, and having before that lived a life of frequent invalidism, Mary Baker Eddy had searched the scriptures to find out what principle Jesus had used to heal. Could it be possible it was still here today, that we were intended to use Jesus' method of healing for all mankind ? Her answer was affirmative.

Many were listening to her message all over the nation. The church in Kansas City conducted services similar to those in Boston and attracted people every Sunday. To Adam Dickey, devoted follower of the empirical, loving, and reforming streams of Methodism, direct descendent of radical, independent-minded Presbyterians, this absolute form of Christ's teachings had to be refreshing. He understood instinctively because it called out to his heart.

On a practical level, he heard that God's children did not need to be slaves to alcohol and tobacco, and, as he later told his own students, he was healed during the class instruction of the use of tobacco. Dickey was a methodical and practical businessman. To him this religion seemed not only inspirational but logical. It could be proved, its adherents claimed, by any "honest seeker of Truth,"as their leader claimed in her book. He later said he went away from those meetings convinced Christian Science was worth a try.

Dickey soon began to test some of the theories on his own, moving from the Methodism he had trusted into a new practicum he could love and prove in his business, family affairs, and life. Trust God as all, turn to Him for daily guidance, and surrender to the knowledge that man is held in total love as a spiritual being, all his affairs ordered. The strains of the family business during this time, with Walter's questionable business practices and the brothers' quarreling over sharing business gains must have given him incentive to look deeper into his spiritual life for satisfying answers.

By 1894 he decided to join The Mother Church which had begun to take form as a beautiful stone edifice in the Back Bay of Boston that very year.Unfortunately, the Dickeys' son Herbert passed on in 1895. It is not known how that affected the father's religious views, but Christian Science's firm teaching on the immortality of the spiritual man must have been comforting.

In 1896 Dickey proceeded to take class instruction from Mrs. Graybill and began practicing Christian Science healing, obtaining gratifying results over the next three years.

Not long after, the church in Kansas City purchased land and began building a permanent structure for First Church of Christ, Scientist, Kansas City, laying the cornerstone December 25, 1897.[3]

Dickey decided to join other Christian Scientists in 1897 in Boston for the Communion Season at The Mother Church. Christian Scientists at that time observed communion only once a year, and it was a time of symbolic spiritual exaltation as well as friendly gathering with those in the fledgling movement. At that year's occasion fourteen-hundred members were added to the church rolls; and they attended along with those who normally came.

This Communion Season Mrs. Eddy issued a surprise invitation for all the visitors to come to her home, Pleasant View.[4] On July 5, 1897, Dickey and two thousand others boarded the train for Concord, New Hampshire, then were transported by a phalanx of horse-drawn vehicles out to Mrs. Eddy's estate.

Pleasant View was a fine but modest-sized country estate. The house, to which Mrs. Eddy had moved in June of 1892 and which she had had renovated, was set on a pretty piece of meadowland to which was later added a scenic pond, orchards, and kitchen gardens that produced yellow raspberries, peas, and sweet corn. The estate included a distinctively painted carriage house and other outbuildings.

Mrs. Eddy appeared on the balcony, escorted by one of her lieutenants, Edward Bates. A few other dignitaries had been invited to join her there, one of them the mayor of Concord. She was dressed exquisitely and wore the diamond cross that became a sort of trademark. She also wore a pin that showed her membership in the Daughters of the American Revolution, possibly to emphasize that this was the day after Independence Day, and—to the surprise of some—a pair of eyeglasses hanging from a gold pin on her gown.

Her cousin, General Henry N. Baker, spoke admiringly of her and her fast-growing religious movement. Judge Septimus J. Hanna of Chicago, now a pillar of the church, spoke eloquently, patriotically comparing Mrs. Eddy to Mollie Stark of New Hampshire, who had assisted her husband, General Stark, at the Battle of Bennington in the Revolution. Other people of reputation who had recently come into Christian Science addressed the crowd. Dickey, like others who reported on the event, must have come away from the meeting with pride in the unfolding destiny of the religion he had joined.

More progressive steps were in order for him in the Christian Science movement. In January of 1898 Mrs. Eddy established the Board of Lectureship of The Mother Church. One of her most effective lecturers, then teacher, was Edward Kimball from Chicago. In June, 1898, he lectured in Kansas City, in what Alfred Farlow of that city described in a June 30 letter to Mrs. Eddy as "a grand success in every way," and "logical, clear and convincing."

When Kimball spoke in Dickey's home city, Dickey may have determined to apply to take advanced class instruction with the lecturer and teacher. His choice was sound. Kimball was considered by Mrs. Eddy and others to be the most effective of all Christian Science speakers. Lectures lasted two hours in those days, and the Kansas City audience was reported to have sat in fascinated silence during the entire event.

Mrs. Eddy said of Kimball at this time that "he does what I require of the Board of Lectureship, persuades and convinces by the logic and the tenderness of Christian Science." Kimball had studied with her in 1888, and she had praised him as a man of common sense, with a fine mind that seized on important things and rejected the trivial. He was straight-forward and able to speak with a simple eloquence that warmed his listeners' hearts.[5]

Kimball and Dickey had much in common. Kimball's background prior to taking up Christian Science was non-academic and not exceptional in terms of social or political prominence. He had established, however, like Dickey, a successful business career, selling lumber and building supplies and had traveled abroad.

Unlike many of his contemporaries in Christian Science, Kimball did not leap immediately into the full-time practice, but learned Christian Science and demonstrated it a bit at a time, along with his wife Kate, in their home city. The couple was personable and answered Mrs. Eddy's need for friendship at times. For example, Kimball told of visiting her while taking class and finding her curled up in a chair, comfy and talkative, wishing life was always that easy.

Dickey must have found the man a charismatic role model. But there was some difficulty in his life outside the religious sphere. The *Kansas City World* reported [March 19, 1898] that he was running for alderman from the 7th Ward, opposed by "Dr. Sawyer, a regular physician." The subject of Dickey's religious preference was being introduced into the campaign. Another unidentified physician stated for the paper:

We are going to organize a club out there which will make its whole object to defeat Dickey. Physicans in this town have been working for years to have sanitary measures [implemented]. Now here comes a man who doesn't believe in any sort of sickness and asks for our votes. He probably considers the entire board of health and city hospital useless and would vote to abolish them. If we did not have the general interests of the people at heart we would help elect the damn fool. It would be a good thing for us doctors.

Dickey retorted in print that it was silly to assume he would vote to abolish a hospital. Another issue in the campaign, according to the newspaper, however, was the death under Christian Science treatment of seven-year-old Mae Kenney, a child in the Seventh Ward. Dickey was probably not the practitioner involved, but the case generated negative comment.[6]

It was just as well that he did not get elected, however. In 1899 affairs at the business in Kansas City were reaching a climax, at least for him. Walter Dickey sent his brother as chief representative for W.S. Dickey Clay Manufacturing Company to Mexico City to discuss plans for the storm and waste sewer systems there, and his wife Lillian accompanied him. Dickey later told his Christian Science students that that night the city's representative, supposed to converse with the representative of Dickey Clay, could not meet. He was suffering from jaundice. The Dickeys agreed he looked terrible.

Politely the husband and wife asked if they might pray for him. Surprised but gratified, he consented. The Dickeys turned to the Bible, to the Christian Science textbook, and to their own prayers, working all night. The next morning the city officer told them he was better. Soon he was healed and asked many questions about Christian Science. By the time they left a little group of citizens had begun reading the Christian Science Bible lessons together. The Dickeys served as First and Second Readers. Eventually this informal group became First Church of Mexico City, the first Christian Science church in Mexico and one of the first outside the United States.[7]

When the couple returned home, they discussed what had happened. They had assisted others before, but this healing seemed to be decisive, pointing in some direction God intended. Dickey decided he should leave the Dickey Clay enterprises and become a full-time Christian Science practitioner. During that year both he and his wife were listed in *The Christian Science Journal.*

The change was not without its challenges. As we have seen, Walter had not allowed his brothers any financial equity, giving them little reward for their service. Adam and his wife had no nest egg and little idea of how they would support themselves without company income.

"Perhaps," Dickey told his wife, "I should keep some part of the job going along with the practice." At this point the couple had eight dollars in their savings account. He decided to accept an offer from the company to return to its service; then, before he could come back for even a day, declined it. Drawn by what he had heard of Edward Kimball, Dickey now applied to him for normal class instruction, so he could himself become a teacher of Christian Science. He was accepted for the 1900 normal class in Boston.

But when he had completed the course, it was determined that only twenty-one graduates could be certified as Christian Science teachers. There was one too many students. Though he was entitled to be certified, he deferred to another student from Kansas City whom he believed had seniority. So he took the class again in Boston in 1901, assuring himself that if the first class had been so wonderful, the second could only be better.

Dickey could have been under no illusions at the time of his attendance at the 1900 Normal Class about the cross currents attending the growth of the religion he was now living. The fact that Christian Science was so successful had thrust it into concentrated national focus in the newspapers, and they more often than not attacked it.

During the previous summer there had been a furor over the vindictive letters-to-editors and articles of Josephine Woodbury, whose court libel case against Mary Baker Eddy had been settled in Mrs. Eddy's favor. The matter was the subject of constant discussion and prayer among students who were already used to odd happenings in their young movement.

The Woodbury case was the affair of the moment in Boston as Dickey came to take, and re-take, class instruction. Josephine Woodbury was an articulate student of Mrs. Eddy's who had gone off the track over a period of ten years. A troubled woman, who had early on shown enthusiasm for, and success in, Christian Science, she had veered into strange practices including black magic, monasticism, and blatant immorality. She created her own little kingdom and finally so outraged her teacher that The Mother Church board excommunicated her.

But Mrs. Woodbury did not take the rejection easily. Noting that Mrs. Eddy had thundered against "The Babylonish Woman" in her communion address of 1899 [*My*, p. 127,] Mrs. Woodbury believed the attack was a personal one on her and brought suit. Lawyers for Mrs. Eddy contended the attack against "the serpent" and the "Babylonish Woman" were intended to indicate a state of murderous and hateful thought, not a reference to a specific person. Courts ruled in favor of Mrs. Eddy. In 1900 and '01, Mrs. Woodbury worked with others to prove that Christian Science had been "stolen" from Phineas Quimby, a mesmeric mental healer who physically manipulated patients and whom Mrs. Eddy had consulted over a period of time.

During this period Christian Science spread into England and Germany, where hundreds of Christian Science healings seemed to indicate a new age. The new magazine, the *Christian Science Sentinel,* included stories on world news as well as metaphysical articles. Those gathering for class knew, and might have spoken, about Mrs. Eddy's foster son, Ebenezer Foster Eddy, who was "fired" from all activities after the last of a series of debacles as First Reader in Philadelphia. It was a sad moment for Mrs. Eddy, who wished her "Benny" to replace son George, who lived in the far West and was not close to her.

Fresh from his inspiring second class with Kimball, Dickey offered instruction in Christian Science in 1901. He was elected First Reader of First Church, Kansas City that year and served again from 1906-1908, continuing to teach and continue the practice of Christian Science there.

His extended family went about their energetic pace, and he never stopped loving them and putting them in a place of honor in his life. By 1908, his siblings were well established in Kansas City and elsewhere, his parents enjoying the fruits of long, good lives in the midst of their children and grandchildren. The Dickey family were high-flying and interesting people, with a restlessness both individual and characteristic of the age.

W.S. Dickey Clay Manufacturing Company continued to implement its dominant position in the United States for manufacture of clay sewer pipe, with Walter using whatever means it took to get there. His son describes the success of the company about 1905, after the departure of its chief salesman Adam Dickey:

> Father was a business, political and civic power in Kansas City and remained just that for the next 20 years. He devoted himself with great zeal, to his varied responsibilities. He had 26 manufacturing plants scattered in 12 states in the South and West with 10 branch offices located in principal cities from Chicago to Atlanta to San Francisco. The Dickey Co. was doing an annual volume of 9 million which gave W.S. a net annual profit of from ¾ of a million to, in some years, $1,250,000.00

Walter Dickey had his eye on a larger arena: civic responsibility which could lead to political office. In the early twentieth century, political office meant power—and bossism. The groundwork involved joining committees, playing golf with important people, and being a prominent local philanthropist. His son writes:

> Walter S. Dickey was a leading citizen. He led in the amount contributed to all charity drives. It was not so much that he was charitable as it was pride in being the largest contributor. The fact was duly chronicled on the front page of the *Star* to his great personal satisfaction. He was automatically placed on all committees for civic uplift and betterment. He was one of the largest stockholders in the National Bank and the Commerce Trust Co, as it was later called, after the banks merged.

Fred Dickey was his brother's right-hand assistant, handling the books and records. The rest of the family went on grumbling about tactics that had driven his brothers Adam, Nathaniel, and Alfred out of the company—and the lack of adequate remuneration. Their father remained a stockholder in some of the enterprises, but he was growing old. There was no one to restrain Walter. Sister Lillian was considering homesteading—somewhere in the West.

Adam Dickey left the business world of his family in 1900, saying goodbye to a corporation that would lead the industry for years. He simply turned his back on it and the win-at-all-costs mentality that dominated the world in which that business functioned.

He had committed heart, soul and pocketbook to Christian Science, and, whatever that commitment implied, he was ready to accept. It would mean many changes from the life already lived. The boy who had avidly read and argued points at debate, and whose memory retained almost all of what he read, would read almost nothing but the Bible and the writings of Mary Baker Eddy for the next fifteen years.

In 1908 he was called to serve the Discoverer and Founder of Christian Science at her home near Boston.

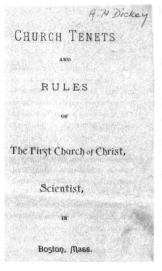

CHURCH TENETS

AND

RULES

OF

The First Church of Christ,

Scientist,

IN

Boston, Mass.

Oɴ the twenty-third day of September, 1892, by advice of our beloved Teacher, Rev. Mary Baker G. Eddy, twelve of her students met and formed a Christian Science Church, and named it The First Church of Christ, Scientist. At this meeting twenty other students of Mrs. Eddy were elected members of this church, which with the twelve who formed the church, are to be known as " First members." Church Tenets formulated by Mrs. Eddy, were adopted, also rules for the government of the church.

The First Church of Christ, Scientist, in Boston, Mass., is designed to be built on the rock, Christ, which includes the understanding and demonstration of Truth and Love ; to represent the church universal and to reflect the church triumphant.

Boston, Mass., *Oct. 18*, 189

Mr. Adam H. Dicke

Kansas City

Mo.

Dear *Brother*: Your app cation to become a member of T First Church of Christ, Scientist in Boston, Mass., has been receiv and you were accepted as a memb of this Church in conformity wi the following Tenets and Rules,

Oct. , 189

Yours fraternally,

William B. Johnson, Cle

Courtesy Keith McNeil Collection

The application form for membership in The First Church of Christ Scientist from Mr. Adam H. Dickey in 1897.

First Church of Christ, Scientist, Kansas City, Missouri, where Mr. Dickey served in various capacities.

Courtesy Longyear Museum Collection

Clay Pipe factory in ca. 1907.

Courtesy Kansas City Public Library

Chapter Four

In the Home of Mrs. Eddy: A Need for a Friendly Ear

Mary Baker Eddy's biographer, Robert Peel, writes that, "To be a member of the Pleasant View household was, according to those who came and went, something between an unremitting discipline and a perpetual revelation."[1]

Adam Dickey was called to become a part of the household in 1908 and was to find Peel's observation true. By the time he arrived, the household had just moved camp to a grander domicile in Chestnut Hill outside Boston, an establishment Mrs. Eddy, quoting Shakespeare, once referred to, as "Oh, Splendid Misery." The call to serve his leader came after he had settled into the life of practitioner and teacher for some six years. Like most others who were asked to help at the household, he considered the call the sort of God-inspired message that Samuel heard as a boy, Abraham heard when he left Ur of the Chaldees, and Moses felt when he was told to lead his people away from Egypt.

Dickey would be joining a select group who had given up almost all they had of personal life. They came to the suburbs of Boston to help in the household of a woman who had few relatives she could count on, few real friends. Mary Baker Eddy had to rely on her own students to perform the most menial duties of daily life. They served as housekeepers, gardeners, even coachmen. They picked the peas in the garden and helped her dress in the morning. And it took more than one personal secretary, which was the job Mrs. Eddy probably had in mind for the bright young man from Kansas City. This bustle of activity carried on by people who were usually strangers to each other when they met created an odd situation never entirely happy for those involved, but at a basic level it worked.

The community Dickey walked into was like a hive of buzzing, sometimes stinging bees, set in a beautiful garden. Here for the first time, he would show the mettle, common sense, and spiritual understanding it would take to help keep the hive from flying apart.

There could be strong challenges in the home of this woman who had articulated Christianity in a new and dynamic form. Hers had been a long path, full of sudden turns of inspiration, leaps of leadership, and pausing points filled with unseen fulfillment. In 1908 she sat at the pinnacle of a career that had taken her from the hard-scrabble soil and wearing farm life of New Hampshire to life as one of the world's most admired women. She was adored by the almost half-million people who formed her congregations worldwide and had the rare distinction in history of being a significant religious founder, like John Calvin, George Fox, and John Wesley. Of women founding religious denominations, one could think of only Mother Ann of the Shakers, and her followers were down to ladies and men of advanced years in slowly dying communities in Kentucky, Maine, and New Hampshire.

There had been many occasions in the 1890s when Mrs. Eddy had gleaned public recognition; papers in Boston and Chicago had been frank to praise the purity and healing results of her movement. Most important, lives had been saved from sin and sickness. Many were the converts, and this more than anything was a continuing satisfaction to her in these later years. The prosperity of the movement, firmly entrenched in the first decade of the twentieth century, made her happy in her reflective moments. Certainly the students' appreciation of Christian Science and its practicable results, she said, gave "the twilight of my years a glow of sunset glory."[2]

But storm clouds often dominated her mood in these latter days as well. A dark side to denominational founding was nothing new. The record for those who brought spiritual enlightenment to humankind is often a grim one. George Fox spent years in a darkened dungeon and died for his faith; Menno Simmons of the Mennonites was killed. John Wesley was miserable, pursued by those who thought he was the Antichrist; Calvin fled Geneva, barely escaping with his life. Mother Ann of the Shakers had to sail to America to escape her persecutors. And tradition says Peter was crucified upside down and Paul executed, following their Master's agonizing death, that of a thief.

Mrs. Eddy was not run out of town or executed. But her existence since she discovered and founded Christian Science meant constant cross-bearing. Her life as leader, she said, was one of "patching breaches widened the next hour, of pounding wisdom and love into sounding brass; of warming marble and quenching volcanoes."

Relatives shunned her. Her sisters, Martha and Abigail, had been alienated from her for years, unable to understand her work. Their quiet, favorite younger sister had metamorphosed into a controversial religious reformer. They had died, Martha in 1884, Abigail in 1886, and although Mary Baker Eddy had not seen them in a long time, memories of both happy early years and later schism remained with her. The press hounded the children of her siblings and cousins, and few of them remained loyal.

The track Mrs. Eddy had left behind her, like footsteps in the snow, had many side-stops and loops: lawsuits against her by former friends who claimed they were unpaid. George Barry, for example, in the 1870s, sued for $2,700 for copying her manuscripts but, in effect, lost his case. Also, a murder case was trumped up by her enemies—husband Gilbert Eddy was arrested and went to jail. A judge acquitted Mr. Eddy after a chief witness admitted he lied. Then there was the passing of that husband, with her own conviction that he had been killed by all the malice of those opposed to Christian Science. But she writes,

> The discoverer of Christian Science finds the path less difficult when she has the high goal always before her thoughts, than when she counts her footsteps in endeavoring to reach it. [S&H, p. 426]

She does not say the footsteps did not come to mind from time to time. Then there were the individuals with odd schemes and bizarre takes on her religion. Many, like the Mrs. Woodbury already referred to, embarrassed the religion, often attempting to dignify their doings by trying to involve their leader, misquoting or inventing speeches "authorized by Mrs. Eddy" and making her sound like a lunatic.

As another example, in the time before Dickey came to live with Mrs. Eddy, Julia Field-King was a successful field representative for Christian Science in England in the mid-1890s, attracting prominent men and women to the movement. She promulgated the socially elite version of Christian Science that threatened to become dominant in Britain, separating it from practice by average citizens.[3]

Under the influence of certain theories prevalent at the turn of the century, Mrs. Field-King enthusiastically announced to Mrs. Eddy that her genealogical studies had found that Mrs. Eddy was among the chosen few of the Anglo-Saxon race whose lineage goes back to King David and the lost tribes of Israel. She showed in her pages of specious genealogy work that Mrs. Eddy was also related to Queen Victoria.

Mrs. Eddy was temporarily taken in, talked about publication of the genealogy, and then, more cautiously, asked that the findings be verified. They were found to be inaccurate. Letter after letter in the collection of the Mary Baker Eddy Library shows her responding to those who wished to initiate similar schemes in their own locales to promote Christian Science, or those who wished to solicit her endorsement of far-out causes, or asked for help in their failing marriages or family squabbles.

Other former students turned on her. During the 80s and 90s and even after the turn of the century, disaffected students dropped away. Not content to depart in silence, they announced their grievances into the ears of a press that trumpeted forth like broadside ballad mongers of Elizabeth I's time the claims of drug taking, doctrine stealing, and outright lying. At times Mary Baker Eddy was accused of being an immoral woman, a forger, a witch, and the Antichrist, all of it in the morning or afternoon newspapers.

Students complained that she was arbitrary, ordering them about like puppets, calling them over in the middle of the night, sending them to Minneapolis or Chicago. Clara Choate, whom she considered the best friend she had during the early 1880s, and one of her most effective healers, complained about the bossiness. But her students and others in the early movement also accused Mrs. Choate of making sexual advances towards men who came to her for help. Other dropouts had their own problems with the rigorous disciplines imposed by the movement's demands for clean conduct and the necessity of obedience to their chief. They were part of a trail that in 1908 stretched into the past for thirty years.

Clergymen, whom Mrs. Eddy had expected to accept her discovery as salutary to Christian practice, had instead piled on from the beginning and continued to "expose" and denounce her and her faith. From the early 80s men of the cloth had reviled Christian Science from the pulpit. Boston University Professor Luther T. Townsend and evangelical minister Reverend A.J. Gordon began the attacks in Boston in 1884 and '85, and clerical disapproval had been strong and vocal through the turn of the century.[4]

It must have been discouraging to read in the newspapers and pamphlets of the day diatribes that often reflected misunderstanding of the basis of Mrs. Eddy's discovery. Though some came to her side, few clergymen attempted to understand what she had been saying.

> The prayer that reforms the sinner and heals the sick is an absolute faith in Him . . . Man, governed by his Maker, having no other Mind—planted on the Evangelist's statement that "all things were made by Him [the Word of God] and without Him was not anything made that was made"—can triumph over sin, sickness and death." [*S&H*, pp.1, 231, 232]

This was radical thinking, not easy of quick acceptance. Traditional Christian religious thought had centered on the person of Jesus, the grace that had sent him to earth, and his mystical mission of salvation through the cross, but did not emphasize the state of cosmic being that lay behind it all and animated his every word and deed. It was that state of being, the ontology back of Jesus' career that informed the Science of Christianity

God, Spirit is all; matter is not ultimately real; Jesus knew that and called upon the all-power of God, Spirit, to triumph over "every ill that flesh is heir to." Mankind, in reality the perfect children of this perfect God, can practice Jesus' healing and salvation from sin and death as scientifically as chemists in the laboratory can produce H^2SO^4 by repeating already proven results from an original hypothesis. We can "go and do likewise." That was what it was all about. A perceptively different understanding of reality.

Rivaling the clergy in misunderstanding and misrepresentation were the "spinoffs" of her discovery. Practicing what was variously called, "mental science," "spiritual science," or "mind healing," these practitioners of a deviant form of the original communicated with each other, set up "healing" practices, advertised, and held conferences. More importantly, they published ersatz and superficial copycat versions of *Science and Health* for their own benefit, like Ursula Gestefeld's 1888 *Statement of Christian Science, Comprised in Eighteen Lessons and Twelve Sections*.[5]

Mrs. Eddy answered in newspapers and articles in *The Christian Science Journal*. She sent letters and protests to those who published, but there was little she could do about these ill informed, but sometimes dangerous, efforts. Copyright violations of her published works continued into the twentieth century and had to be checked constantly by both lawyers and those on the home staff. Her setting up in the *Church Manual* committees on publication was intended to counterattack vicious or ignorant misrepresentation head-on.

The harassment continued during Mrs. Eddy's last decade, at a time when, ironically, the movement was flourishing as never before. It was, in the course of things, passing from an inspirational, charismatic leadership to another form—an institutional framework that would take it into the future. Daily concerns about business and spiritual directions occupied most of her waking hours. Meetings with her editors, with teachers and practitioners who were expanding the movement, and with leaders in the building of the physical church demanded all her energies without the distractions of a hostile press.

Workers arrived at and left the home, some from quite humble origins like Anna Machacek, whom Peel describes as a Bohemian immigrant who entered the household as laundress, became head of housekeeping, and eventually left to become a Christian Science practitioner in Chicago. Others abandoned flourishing practices in big cities to serve. Calvin Frye came in the 1880s and stayed for over twenty years. Idealistic young women who had joined the movement and become practitioners answered the call and served, surprised at the amount of time and detail the job demanded, but amazed at the spontaneous teaching and Bible enlightenment they received from their "boss" while they were dusting the knick-knacks.

Some of the household later wrote of their experiences, and in spite of all the demands and unusual night prayer vigils and the inner dissensions natural to a group in an intense situation—all testified to the spiritual steadfastness of the leader.

No matter what the apparent "attacks" in the dark of night, no matter how overloaded her day by the cares of the movement, Mary Baker Eddy stood firmly planted on the truths of her discovery. It taught that trusting God and spiritual intuition—trusting the insights that came from God, the divine Mind that encompasses all reality—saw one through even the most discouraging moments. Often she wrote during this period that she had no doubt that Spirit, the source of her own and everyone's being, would inform her, instruct her, lead her into true and meaningful paths. And "let no mortal interfere with God's government by thrusting in the laws of erring, human concepts." [*S&H*, p. 62:24]

The meaning of the household experience—the life of Mary Baker Eddy at home during her last five difficult years—is vital to understanding her. This fact was not always easily accepted. For years the board of directors believed the details were "too human." That she was remarkably alert and on top of business affairs into her eighties, that she met visitors in a poised manner and was genuinely interested in their lives, that she ran her church and household with attention to detail—that was one thing. But that she was sometimes discouraged, sometimes in pain tormented by a physical problem, sometimes seeming arbitrary and cranky to members of the board and others delegated to handle some of her affairs—that could not be talked about.

But her spirituality in the face of multiple challenges was the bedrock of the household experience. The human "Mary," as she called herself when she had weak moments, cried out for succor, human love, relief from care, and peace. That had been true for years; her correspondence to both those who knew her and casual acquaintances had been loaded with yearning to be understood.

Still, human empathy and understanding would not answer the heart's deep needs. Only reaffirmation of the inviolable unity of God with the perfect and eternal self could bring harmony. So in these days of fulfillment of her church, as a stone Extension arose in the Back Bay to add to the original Mother Church of the denomination built a few years before, as thousands of new adherents each month predicted a permanent future for The Mother Church, in the household she stood essentially alone with her God.

She had come to the point of absolute reliance on Him through many trials, and she was not about to bend. It took this spiritual firmness to thrust the movement forward. During the years 1888 and 1889, after a rebellion of Boston students, she had closed the Massachusetts Metaphysical College and dissolved the traditional structure of the Church of Christ, Scientist. After that, she had prepared for a different form of church, and it was this process that was fully maturing just before 1908 when Adam Dickey arrived.

She wrote in the *Church Manual*:

The First Church of Christ, Scientist, in Boston, Mass, is designed to be built on the Rock, Christ, even the understanding and demonstration of divine Truth, Life and Love, healing and saving the world from sin and death; thus to reflect in some degree the Church universal and triumphant.

Human wisdom had failed her repeatedly. Difficulties were not going away in the twilight of her life. But she would not deviate from reliance on God only. Would those around her own home understand?

Dickey on more than one occasion gave his friends and readers a statement he believed in unwaveringly. "God is all there is. When you have said that, you have said all there is to say." This essential message, which sounds much like the central theme of many of Mrs. Eddy's letters during this period, is what he would need to rely on as he stepped into the household at Chestnut Hill.

Chapter Five

Inside "Splendid Misery"

Adam Dickey's summons to Chestnut Hill was probably the most momentous happening of his life.[1]

He tells the story in his *Memoirs of Mary Baker Eddy*, published in the 1920s.

> During the year 1907, while serving as First Reader in First Church Christ, Scientist, Kansas City, Missouri, I received a call from a gentleman from Boston, who spent a few hours, Sunday afternoon, in our home. He informed me of the nature of his errand in Kansas City, which was to the effect that he was looking for people to go to Concord, New Hampshire, to live in the home of Mrs. Eddy and there to serve her in different capacities.

> He explained to me that it was difficult for our Leader to find suitable persons to assist in her household. When she needed a personal maid, there were always plenty of volunteers, but very few who could pass the requirements. The same situation existed in regard to other work in the household, difficulty in finding persons to do necessary cooking, serving, and other general tasks.

> I was informed, then, that Mrs. Eddy had quite a large household and that those serving in any capacity in her home came under a line of malpractice that existed nowhere else on earth. The difficulty of discovering people who would meet the requirements and who possessed the necessary qualifications for performing this work for our Leader made it necessary for the Directors, acting under Mrs. Eddy's instructions, to appoint a committee whose sole purpose was to scour the country, if need be, in order to find suitable persons. Our Leader in her great work for humanity found it necessary that her time and thought

be fully given to the work in hand, and that she should not be occupied or annoyed with petty details of household management. The members of this committee, usually three in number, of which my caller was at that time the traveling representative, interviewed many people in their effort to find any who were qualified to perform this work. They must be willing to leave homes and friends and take up their residence in the home of our leader . . ..

Our leader was very strict in her requirements. For instance, if one had formerly suffered from a belief that had incapacitated him, even though he had been healed and restored apparently to perfect health, she did not want such a person in her house.

The reason Mrs. Eddy was so specific about her employees was that she had found that the vulnerable became targets.

The visitor, who may have been John Lathrop, told Dickey and his wife that though it might seem intrusive that investigations should be made about prospective workers, Mrs. Eddy wanted to be very scrupulous. Dickey goes on to explain that he told the visitor he knew of no one who would answer the needs of a personal maid, the position open at the time.

Shortly after [this interview,] I visited Boston, in June of 1907, to attend the communion service and Annual Meeting. Here again I met the student who had called upon me in the west, and for the first time learned that whole time he was quizzing me about other people, who might be employed to work for Mrs Eddy, he was quietly sizing me up as a possible choice for an assistant in Mrs. Eddy's home in connection with secretarial work. While in Boston on this occasion I was invited to step into the Treasurer's office, which at that time was in The Mother Church, and there I was interviewed by a committee of three. They questioned me quite closely with regard to my own work and the length of time I had been in Science, and what I felt I had accomplished and then asked me if I would be willing to respond to a call from the Directors, in case they should see fit to invite me to work in Mrs. Eddy's home. I told them I had no higher aim in life than to be of service to Mrs. Eddy and the Cause of Christian Science and that if they needed somebody to shovel the snow off her front sidewalk, I would drop everything else and give all my time to her service in any capacity whatever.

The directors laughed and told him they did not have much difficulty getting people to shovel snow. Could he type? Yes, he could. They would be in touch. On January 29, 1908, he received a special delivery letter from the directors of The Mother Church that asked him to come to Boston immediately.

> Mr. Adam H. Dickey, C.S.B.
> The New York
> 12th and Paseo
> Kansas City, Mo.
> Dear Brother:
> The Directors hereby extend to you a loving call to serve our beloved leader, the Rev. Mary Baker Eddy, according to the terms of the By-law Article XXII, Section 10 of the *Church Manual.*
>
> If you will come sooner than the ten days, it will be very much appreciated.
>
> As soon as you can after receiving this letter, will you please telegraph me at what time you will be in Boston? And upon your arrival, call me by telephone at Back Bay 1470 between the hours of 8:00 and 12:AM and 1:00 and 5:00 PM and at Back Bay 1506 at other times.
>
> Very Sincerely Yours
>
> William B. Johnson, Secretary

Another influential Christian Scientist had recommended Dickey in a letter of January 24, 1908. Daisette Stocking McKenzie, one of Mrs. Eddy's most loyal and respected students, had written to her asking her to consider Dickey for a secretary's position, emphasizing his healing work.[2]

Dickey thought he would need to stay for a year, based on his knowledge of the by-law in the *Manual.* He packed his trunk and headed to the railroad station after a final appearance at the Reader's desk in his home church. He had wondered how he would break the news of his position to the church members and to the clients he was helping as a practitioner. But he did not feel he could reveal confidential correspondence, so decided he would tell them after arriving in Boston. Lillian had not been invited.

As Dickey boarded the train in Kansas City, he had much to think about—besides the burden of the family he was leaving behind. The leader would be glad for a responsible businessman who could serve her in some management capacity. He was not sure what he would be called upon to do, but his experience and temperament would surely be helpful. He knew of some of the challenges of her daily schedule, but not of their extent.

During the previous few years, Mary Baker Eddy had been recognized as a great spiritual figure, with public awards and inclusions in book collections of notable people. People from all walks of life and areas of America, both Christian Scientists and non-Scientists, asked to have interviews. Her universal reply was that she could not see anyone; her work took all her time. To one importuning clergyman she finally wrote in September, 1906:

> Should I give myself the pleasant pastime of seeing your personal self, or give you the opportunity of seeing mine, you would not see me thus, for I am not there. . . Those who look for me in person or elsewhere than in my writings lose me instead of find me. [My, p. 120]

She stayed at home, occupied with the demanding routine of writing, editing, and running her church with its expanding publishing activities. Each day she cherished a carriage ride out of the house, but even here she sometimes shielded herself with a parasol when people stared. Her sense of seclusion had grown after a painful and notorious article appeared in McClure's Magazine a year and a half earlier, before Dickey was called. This muckraking periodical had determined to "expose" her and for some time had been interviewing old acquaintances and others to reveal her a charlatan.

A journalist whose career and identity are still shadowy, Georgine Milmine, had gathered the information. The articles she wrote based much of their negativity on interviews with a Frederick Peabody, an avowed Eddy-hater and with other of her enemies. Editors at the magazine, including Willa Cather, refined the articles into a series of vicious attacks. Even then, the thinness of the accusations was noted by many, but it has only been in our own time that most of the attackers have been shown as falsifying, agenda-driven, and seeking retribution for alleged slights. Nevertheless, the Christian Science world was shaken by the articles, and many who did not know Mrs. Eddy believed the charges of her stealing others' work and misrepresenting herself.

New York's Joseph Pulitzer joined the hounds by deciding to find out if the woman were even alive. Two reporters came to Pleasant View to meet Mrs. Eddy and seemed satisfied that she was healthy and sound of mind, then wrote a sensational article that she was dying, impersonated by her maid on her carriage rides, and that Calvin Frye had taken over her estate and business affairs. Other demands for interviews, stories about failing health, and opposing, vindicating stories appeared, no doubt taking their toll on the household and what should have been Mrs. Eddy's peaceful retirement years.

On his way to the Chestnut Hill household, Dickey must have looked forward to seeing the impressive Extension to the original Mother Church completed two years before. During the 1902 effort to raise funds for it, he and Lillian had withdrawn their last $2,000 from their savings account and sent it to Boston.

He knew that back of some of the mystery surrounding Mrs. Eddy in the eyes of the world was the personality of Calvin Frye, a man with whom he would soon be coming into daily contact. Frye seemed to control everything in her life: screening her mail, admitting or denying whomever he wanted to let in, or keep out of the house, apparently organizing just about everything she did.

Earlier, Frye's position at Pleasant View along with other complaints was alleged as a cause for Mrs. Eddy's son, George Glover, Jr., to join others to bring suit to see if his mother was, indeed, incapacitated, and herself and her fortune under the control of others. The legal action was called the "Next Friends Suit."

Mrs. Eddy was, after all, reaching her late eighties. There were times when her hands might shake, her voice sound less than strong. She admitted she needed to listen carefully to hear conversation. In addition, a physical problem from time to time caused her pain. Yet those who visited her commented on her graceful carriage, clarity of thought, and favorable appearance. The suit's plaintiffs, bringing their action through her vulnerable and not-too-worldly-minded son, pressed on to try to prove that she was incapable and that her finances should be placed in other hands.

Dickey would have known that just the previous August 14, 1907, court officers had visited Mrs. Eddy at Pleasant View and found that she answered their questions fully and competently. After that, the Next Friends Suit seemed nothing but frivolous. The plaintiffs moved for dismissal themselves. She had been forgiving and temperate in her reactions, settling substantial sums on both her son and her adopted son, "Benny" Foster-Eddy, in return for their promises not to contest her will, which left her money to her church—a promise they did not keep.

Dickey might have looked forward to seeing his teacher when he arrived at his new home, but Kimball was no longer in Boston. He and Mrs. Eddy had had a split of sorts, probably necessitated in part by Kimball's growing personal popularity and the intensity of his teaching method—and also by Mrs. Eddy's sincere concern that those on the Board of Education should be rotated much as she had insisted that the First Reader of The Mother Church should rotate out. In a letter dated November 26, 1903, she wrote that Kimball should not teach so much as heal. Mrs. Eddy had been disappointed in the quality of healing in the field and said teaching was not needed so much as better healing. "I think. . . it best for you not to locate in Boston, and for the sake of Truth to teach in the board but two classes annually." Kimball had acquiesced graciously, but he had been hurt. He would return to full-time lecturing. Much of this would have been known by Dickey as he proceeded on his way from Kansas City to Boston.

One changed trains in Chicago to travel to Boston. Looking at his watch, Dickey realized he had a little time before the Boston train left.

> Having been unable to purchase a copy of the latest "Manual" in Kansas City, before leaving, I visited the Reading Room, a magnificently furnished apartment on the top floor of a building on South Michigan Ave. I did not make myself known to the Librarian, but observing a consignment of new "Manuals" which had just arrived, I purchased one and turned to Article XXII, Section II. Somewhat to my surprise I saw that the wording had been changed, so that the person accepting the call, instead of remaining with Mrs. Eddy for one year, unless she requested otherwise, the By-law read, should remain for three years.

The by-law change had actually been made in 1905 in the 49th edition of the *Manual*. He took in the new information with aplomb. "My thoughts were buoyant and hopeful and I felt that no greater blessing could fall to me than to receive such a call," he said as he detailed the experiences in his *Memoirs*.

Falling snow covered the entire countryside as he traveled east. Trains were delayed, and traffic slowed. Finally, at 11 o'clock in the evening, rather than at the expected hour of 3 PM, Mr. Dickey from Kansas City climbed down from the train. He called the operator, reached the number in Back Bay, and was told to check into a hotel and to be ready at 6:30 in the morning to drive out to the stone mansion and property known as Chestnut Hill. Mrs. Eddy had moved into this home just weeks before, her bags and entourage taken by a special train without fanfare to avoid the public eye.

She had called for the move in July before the Next Friends Suit was to be heard in court. It is said that she lost trust in the laws of New Hampshire, the place of the suit, and believed the laws of Massachusetts would better protect her. She thought ahead carefully about the floor plan and furnishings at the new estate. "I want a window in my room like the one here," she wrote in September to the board and followed with another message, part of the soft refrain often sounded in that era of her life, "It relieves my lonely hours."[3]

When she arrived, Mrs. Eddy found the house less to her liking than she'd hoped. It was a huge mausoleum of a place, like a Roman palace with Victorian woodwork. Her own study was too big and—not cozy. She immediately called for modifications and moved to the third floor of the house while remodeling went on.

Entering the front hall and having been ushered into the dining room, Dickey found breakfast in progress with Frye presiding as head of the table

He was invited to join the staff, but the group seemed a little less than welcoming. They were distracted, aloof. Only the temporary secretary had anything much to say to him.

The staff had been much beset during the past two years, and especially the last six months. The move to Chestnut Hill was not as easy a matter of business as the recruiter who spoke to him at the communion had suggested. Many of the household and clerical staff, Joseph Mann for one, had departed on urgent personal business. One worker who had received negative attention in Pulitzer's *New York World* attack, Pamelia Leonard, had become seriously ill, left, and died just three weeks prior to Dickey's arrival. And publisher Joseph Armstrong, a specially targeted enemy of lawyers in the Next Friends Suit, had died a month earlier. As if that were not enough, the pioneering Christian Scientist Irving Tomlinson's delicate sister Mary, in the very midst of the Next Friends lawsuit, had suffered a mental breakdown and thrown herself to her death out of the Parker House Hotel.

Their leader was aging, under dire attack, and the movement seemed to be collapsing around them, a house undermined by flood waters. They eyed each other suspiciously. Who would be the next to leave, and what blows would mortal mind next deliver? They stayed "with their books," uplifting thought, and ventured only rarely into open friendships.

Mrs. Eddy was tougher. She simply decided they needed to move and after they were settled, that most of all, the entire operation needed steady, business-like hands at the helm to assist her in steering the ship through troubled waters. Everybody had best be up to "praying without ceasing"; that was the need of the moment. Enter Adam Dickey.

> After meeting Mr. Frye, I was introduced to Mrs. Laura Sargent, whom I already knew, and to three other members of the household including the gentleman who was serving temporarily as secretary to Mrs. Eddy. After breakfast he told me many things about Mrs. Eddy's household that were new and interesting to me.

The secretary, Arthur Reeves Vosburg,[4] was the only person in the house who gave a clue as to what he was supposed to do. There had been many comings and goings; the staff believed it was wise to be cautious and let newcomers prove themselves before getting too close because Mrs. Eddy fired people without ceremony when they did not measure up.

Frye inquired if Mr. Dickey had experienced much snow on his way, and Dickey told him he had. The reply came, "We must tell Mother about that." The new arrival wondered why snow should be of interest to Mrs. Eddy but found out later that she did not like heavy snowstorms around her and believed it proper to pray about the weather.[5] The household workers needed always to be on guard against the attacks of "error," which Mrs. Eddy often called evil, and to Mrs. Eddy a drift blocking her doorstep was error. The workers should have prayed about disabling snow around the neighborhood. It was another thing if the snow was nation-wide; the workers could breathe a sigh of relief, Dickey recorded.

Frye, Dickey learned, was a man to be reckoned with. He had worked in Lynn, Massachusetts, in a shoe factory when he had visited a Christian Science service, become interested in the subject, and taken class with Mrs. Eddy in 1881, an early date. He had been with her almost twenty-five years, had seen her, himself, and the household through both triumphs and tragedies.

> He was quiet, even to taciturnity—extremely non-communicative, and with an abruptness in his short answer that might have given the impression to a stranger that he was impatient with his questioner . . . long association with [Mrs. Eddy] had taught him to mind his own business and he expected others to do the same.

Dickey described Frye as a "factotum," who when he was first with Mrs. Eddy fired the furnace and shined the shoes. He moved with her to Concord, where he began driving her about on her afternoon outings and eventually became so trusted that he did her accounts and served as household cashier. The interim secretary advised Dickey in a whisper, "If I were you I would cultivate Frye." Frye could be difficult at times, but Dickey knew how to get along; dealing with his own family had taught him that, and he intended to do so. John. V. Dittemore in a biography of those years said Frye resented "Mr. Dickey," believing he flattered Mrs. Eddy.[6]

On the other hand, Dickey discovered Laura Sargent to be kind and helpful. She had shown Lillian and Adam Dickey through the "Mother's Room" at The Mother Church the year before and had made a favorable impression on them.

The secretary pro-tem took him on a tour of the Chestnut Hill mansion, and Dickey describes it as follows:

> Many, who have visited Mrs. Eddy's home since her departure, will remember it as a large stone structure, massive in its lines. The front door opens from a porte-cochère into a vestibule, and thence into a large hall, which extends to the rear of the house, leading through French doors on to a balcony overlooking a wide expanse of territory, with the Blue Hills in the distance. On the right of the hall are two large rooms, the front one of which was used as the library, and the rear one as a din-

ing room. Between these two rooms is a small transverse hall, leading out to the side door and the kitchen, which is crossed through large openings in which are hung heavy portières. The windows in the dining room also look out over the rear of the estate toward the Blue Hills.

On the left of the front hall is an aperture, or little hall, about ten feet square in which stands the stately hall clock, surrounded by the Ambrose coat of arms of our leader's family. From this antechamber one enters the large drawing rooms extending from the front to the rear and giving an idea of space and expansion to the whole house. In these rooms tastefully displayed are many beautiful rugs, paintings and other ornaments, which have been presented to our leader from time to time by her devoted followers.

He goes on to talk about the balcony off the dining room and drawing room at the back of the house and to say that the home had recently been carpeted throughout and carefully furnished. Someone with taste who belonged to The Mother Church had aided in designing the rooms.

They went up the stairs, and Dickey found his room, not far from Mrs. Eddy's.

I found it equipped as an office, as well as a bedroom. There were house telephones connecting with every room in the house except those occupied by Mrs. Eddy. The room was large, light, airy and well furnished. My guide soon seated himself with me at the desk and began to give me an outline of what my duties were to be.

The secretary pointed to the desk, on which many letters had piled up, awaiting answers. The work would begin right away! For a while Dickey would open the mail. It was necessary to get acquainted with Mrs. Eddy's daily routine: breakfast, receive and read mail, luncheon, usually a carriage ride, and so forth—all of which was rigorously carried out at her wishes.

On that introductory day, as soon as Adam Dickey began to look at the mail that had just arrived, he had word from a member of the household that Mrs. Eddy wished to speak to him.

I think my heart gave a few extra flutters, for this was to me the supreme moment in my Christian Science career. I arose and followed him. He led me along the upstairs hall from the front of the house, diagonally across to a large room at the left and rear which was occupied by Mrs. Eddy as a study . . . .. Mrs. Eddy motioned me to a chair, and we had our first conversation. She was a woman of rather below medium height, slender and having the appearance of a person between eighty and ninety years of age. Her complexion was clear and her eyes were bright. She talked with a most beautifully modulated voice. At times, when she was saying some unusually impressive thing, it took on qualities deep and orotund. It seemed like one of the best trained voices I had ever heard.

He noticed the daintiness and neatness of her attire. She was wearing the well known cross of diamonds at her throat. Dickey observed that she seldom appeared in the same dress on successive days and that she manicured her own nails.

She asked her secretarial candidate about his birthplace and schooling and under what circumstances he had come into Christian Science. She took special interest in the fact that he came from "a family of nine children and two parents all of whom were still alive, that he had never been seriously sick." She dismissed him to his room, where he sat briefly, when four bells rang, and Frye came in. "Mr. Dickey, that is your sign. Whenever you hear four bells, it means for you to respond at once."

Mrs. Eddy wanted to continue their conversation on a deeper basis. She told him that as leader of a successful movement, she had made many enemies, and she was having to combat their influence. "This seemed a very startling disclosure at the time, but nevertheless I accepted it," Dickey writes.

During this and the following days, he mused that he had always believed Mrs. Eddy lived in comfort in her sunset years, much loved and cared for and at peace behind the walls of her lovely home. Most people thought that way.

But the picture he found was quite different.

It was generally believed among Mrs. Eddy's followers that she stood erect physically and mentally at all times and simply spoke the word to error and it would entirely disappear. There were occasions when she did rise to this height, but there were also times when she seemed to bend beneath the heavy load that mortal mind had placed upon her, and it was then that she really yearned for human aid and sympathy.

That Mrs. Eddy "had her moments" was a revelation to him; it would have been to the thousands of followers, also. Only those in the house at Chestnut Hill knew of the heavy load she bore: enemies attacking both her and the faith, weakness sometimes of body, but not of spirit.

Immediately he saw what the "recruiter" had spoken of when he said that malicious animal magnetism seemed to attack in Mrs. Eddy's household more strongly than anywhere else. It was the malignant spirit the entire household had to combat, and it figured greatly in the atmosphere of her last years.

Chapter Six

Evil, Or Malicious Animal Magnetism

Many Christian Scientists of the period spent a good deal of time wrestling with a teaching called "animal magnetism." Dickey dealt with the subject both during his residency at Chestnut Hill and later in his work for the board of The Mother Church, when he had to try to put it in place for the whole movement. It was also fascinating to the public at large and the press, who could be counted on to misrepresent it.

Mrs. Eddy's basic conclusions about what she called animal magnetism were based on her own observation of the ways of the world. When leaders or average men take stands for truth, they almost always draw down evil, or error's penalty. A step forward in clarifying the good and true in life could mean an attack. And the question then became, how should one defend oneself and the cause of truth? Dickey seemed to resolve the problem for his own understanding while he was under Mrs. Eddy's roof; others struggled for entire lifetimes to do so.

She devoted a chapter in *Science and Health* to the subject, entitled "Animal Magnetism Unmasked." The chapter is introduced by a verse from the Bible: "For out of the heart proceed evil thoughts, murders, adulteries, fornications, thefts, false witness, blasphemies: these are the things which defile a man.—Jesus"

The chapter begins with the author's tracing the career of Mesmer, who taught that a force in nature "could be exerted by one living organism over another, as a means of alleviating disease." [*S&H*, p. 100: 4-6] She shows that Mesmer believed the planets and the earth exert forces on human bodies. Mesmerism in the nineteenth century became equated with hypnotism, acting on both mind and body through control of the mind.

Mrs. Eddy believed that the power of animal magnetism, the hypnotic control of one human mind over another, could also impersonally stand for all the works of evil. Even though she emphatically declared that God's eternal all-power as Spirit ruled out evil as reality—in fact, it was the central premise of the practice of Christian Science—she allowed that there was a

suppositional opposite. As long as people accepted the power of evil's hypnotic suggestions, they would seem real and cause sin and suffering.

The suggestions could seem quite tangible, she believed, and were the
cause of all of the trouble the world labored under. And things might grow
worse, because the world did not understand the need to turn to the all-
power of God and reject the malevolent side of human life, the suggestions
of animal magnetism.

> The mild forms of animal magnetism are disappearing,
> and its aggressive features are coming to the front. The looms of
> crime, hidden in the dark recesses of mortal thought, are every
> hour weaving webs more complicated and subtle. So secret are
> the present methods of animal magnetism that they ensnare the
> age into indolence, and produce the very apathy on the subject
> which the criminal desires. [S&H, p. 102: 16-23]

Though this passage may bring to mind *fin de siecle* London with its
dim streets and sinister villains, she intends it to point to the experiences of
fearful mortal thought that all have experienced. Robert Peel called animal
magnetism "entrenched materialism," and "Mrs. Eddy's equivalent of original sin." Or it can be seen simply as resistance to spirituality.[1]

Other denominations traditionally called this sort of dark thinking
and temptation "the devil;" Jesus branded it that way, but he also said the
devil was a "lie and the father of it." Christian Science does not accept
dualism; therefore, evil must be seen as an imposition, a lie, unreality in a
world where God, good, is all. Mrs. Eddy writes, "Mankind must learn that
evil is not power. Its so-called despotism is but a phase of nothingness."
[S&H, p.102:30, 31] That is the central and only real fact about animal
magnetism.

Still, there was a clear dilemma in early Christian Science where animal magnetism was concerned, especially the aggressive, malicious kind.
The movement was under constant, virulent attack. One could see how
strongly it was felt; though powerless from an absolute point of view, it
nevertheless appeared to exert harm and pain. No better example existed
than the founder of Christian Science. There has been no other woman in
American history so maligned.

In an age where religious matters went to American hearts more directly than they do today, Mrs. Eddy had been battered for almost forty years
by some of the very people she cared about, and whom she wanted to love
her. The virtue was that at all times she relied on God for emotional support. But still, she felt she had to be constantly on guard.

It has to be admitted that the early students of Christian Science and
the leader herself seemed to live in a rarified atmosphere where small things

became large, the work-a-day world far off. Odd or unstable people were sometimes attracted and then fell away, drawing notoriety to themselves. Living in this intense atmosphere encouraged a sense of isolation among some of the students, something near to paranoia. Many of these Christian Science pioneers made their own little world, reinforced beliefs and fantasies among themselves, and seemed at times like characters in theatre of the absurd.

And here was their dilemma: If God is All and evil has no reality, then why were they constantly battling an imaginary power called malicious animal magnetism? Mrs. Eddy herself announced that unless it was confronted and shown to be nothing, evil or error would continue to flaunt itself. Work must be done; animal magnetism must be shown to be a lie, powerless. She titled the chapter "Animal Magnetism Unmasked." It needed to be unmasked, and that was the rationale for constant prayer, or as the Scientists called it, "metaphysical work."

Though Mrs. Eddy had staunchly fought malicious animal magnetism for years, including at the time of the passing of her husband, Gilbert Eddy, when she insisted that a kind of mental murder had been committed, her last ten years saw the height of attacks against her movement. At times work against "M.A.M." came to almost dominate the household day and night.

Dickey writes in his *Memoirs* that when he was first approached by someone recruiting him, the student said that only those who were in sound health themselves and free of problems could be considered for the household.

> As soon as the individual entered Mrs. Eddy's employ he came under a certain malicious mental malpractice that he had never encountered before, and our leader was unwilling to subject anybody to this trial, who might be liable to a relapse or return to a diseased belief.

He went on to say that as he got to know the situation he saw that:

> everyone who was in Mrs. Eddy's home was there because of his ability to work and perform the tasks that were set for him. Many people seemed to be inspired with a belief that there could be no pleasanter occupation in the world than to work for Mrs. Eddy. They failed to realize that what Mrs. Eddy wanted and actually required of those about her was the mental support which she found necessary to receive from students in order that she might be uninterrupted in her work for her Cause and for mankind. Mrs. Eddy was at the head of a great Movement, a Church that had grown up under divine direction and was designed, eventu-

ally, to destroy all evil and bring to suffering humanity a remedy for every form of sickness and sin. The same form of evil that attacked the work of Jesus and cried out, "What have we to do with thee, thou Jesus of Nazareth? Art thou come to destroy us?" (Mark 1:24) was by no means lacking in connection with Mrs. Eddy's experience. She was in a position somewhat similar to that of the general of a large army, who is fighting for its existence. The attacks of the enemy would be made, if possible, on the leader of the defending army. . . she needed to be surrounded by the best workers she could find, who virtually acted as a bodyguard and a protection for her in order that she might be able to give her undivided attention to the work necessary to properly safeguard her church.

Impersonal malicious animal magnetism was the attacker, and those at Chestnut Hill stood prayer watches during the night and often during the day to defend her and her cause so that she could go forward with decisions that moved the Christian Science Church forward.

Sensitive to mental insinuations and intuitions, worn by the years of bitter attack, and ever on the alert for the movement she loved, she made handling malicious animal magnetism a priority. Often she called workers to her room at midnight to take up the cudgel against it, especially when she was enduring physical suffering. A telling detail is the fact that a box of Adam Dickey's personal effects, containing materials from the Chestnut Hill years, had at its bottom a layer of little pieces of memo paper, each of which said only "M.A.M." and was signed "MBE."

The battle against malicious animal magnetism was one component of the low spirits Dickey found at Chestnut Hill. The Next Friends Suit had taken its toll, with the illnesses and death among close associates that followed it, but more than that was the realization that Mrs. Eddy would not always be with them. That she had her own crosses to bear with "the belief of aging" she openly acknowledged .

The situation of the household friends was complicated. It was Peter Pan's Neverland in some ways. Thousands of naïve followers from New York to California to Europe and now Asia apparently believed Mrs. Eddy would never die. They had never seen her, knew only of her books and the woman as a living legend. Some presumably thought she simply would be an older woman for hundreds of years, never visited with pain or physical decline; many thought she would be resurrected should she seem to pass from this world. At Chestnut Hill they knew differently, and this was a burden to bear, especially since there were few to speak to about it.

The "yellow" periodicals, greedy and devoid of ethics as they tended to be, posed a question a good deal of America was asking: It was "Who is Mrs. Eddy?" That someone, especially a woman who came from modest circumstances, could be raised to a position of spiritual and temporal power within a generation seemed a phenomenon impossible to explain.

Not everyone saw Mrs. Eddy's achievement as inexplicable and threatening. That she had studied the Bible and prayed with deep enough inspiration to have found the laws of God's reality behind Christ Jesus' teaching—laws that worked to bless and heal mankind—was enough for many, both in and out of the religion.

But for those hostile to religion or to women in power or to success beyond the predictable, another answer bounced around. To them, she was a charlatan, a fraud from the beginning, deceiving for money and power, with out-of-control emotions driving her on in an insatiable lust for personal domination. Since nobody saw her often at this point, anything seemed possible. Maybe the organizational superstructure was holding a comatose Mrs. Eddy up like a mummer's parade dummy—or maybe she was dead already and some woman was impersonating her on those carriage rides through her neighborhood. These strange scenarios had been floated by the *New York World* and by *McClure's Magazine*. The cutting satire in Mark Twain's recent book, *Christian Science*, depicted her as a stupid old bag.

But an ardent minority of her own followers had another answer to the question Paul asks Ananias in the words of the old gospel song ("What kind of man this Jesus is?"). They thought she was the second Christ. She might rise from the dead when, and if, the time came.

Looking at the passages in Revelation that depicted a woman wearing a crown of seven stars with a little book in her hand, they saw Mary Baker Eddy from Bow, New Hampshire. Prominent Christian Scientists, even practitioners and teachers, either hinted at it or said it blatantly: this immaculately pure woman who can cure the sick with a glance was a saint. She was the promised "second messenger."

But almost nothing on earth made Mrs. Eddy's hackles rise more than the assumption she was infallible, a personalization of the Christ-Truth that she insisted was impersonal.

Reverend Joseph Adams, who had been taught by Mrs. Eddy, said in *The Chicago Christian Scientist II* periodical October, 1888:

> If there was one thing she impressed upon our mind, while passing through her classes more than another, it was this, not to look at Mrs. Eddy but the Truth which she declared.[2]

There are many similar accounts, most directly from her, that she not be turned into a "dagon" or object of worship. She knew the dangers of the mental atmosphere such thinking could create and would have none of it. Her rebuke could be sharp when adulation became a smothering blanket.

Annie Dodge, a loyal student, had hoped to help her teacher recover from the smarts of the Next Friends Suit by sending her a glowing tribute that verged on apotheosis:

Mrs. Eddy replied:

> Your letter. . .was astounding. You, that once was calm and wise in your labors for Christian Science, writing like a maniac, more than a Scientist! You an idolater making a god of me! In my article, Personal Contagion, I denounced deeply just what you said in your letter of me beware . . . in turning to a person instead of divine Principle to help in time of need. O that you are blind to this sin seems to be incredible.[3]

Students could not seem to realize that to the woman who valued the First Commandment above all others, their taking her as some sort of demigod before the true and omnipotent Mind was blasphemy—and a terrible burden on her personally.

Those in the household knew well that Mrs. Eddy "in mortal terms" was not such a figure. The older lady calling in the night for various kinds of help and making demands on the staff that sometimes seemed peremptory was like other grandmothers being cared for at home. That was true even if she was one of the best known women in the nation, whose touched-up photo had been reverently placed on the walls of thousands of living rooms, like "Jesus at the Door of the Heart."

So one of the cross-currents Adam Dickey found at Chestnut Hill was the "Second Messenger" view of the leader. She had, after all, demanded that a proper view of her be a requirement for fully understanding and expressing Christian Science. What did that mean if not divine status? The answer should have been obvious. Proper view meant crediting her with her discovery, not looking at Eastern religions or manipulative healer Phineas Quimby as the progenitor of her works.

But there was more to it; her distrust of adulation was grounded in the knowledge that to treat her as a saint was to ignore the difficulties it had taken, and was still taking, to nurture the movement.

Probably above all she wanted her students to understand the suffering that had occurred to bring Christian Science to the world. It was that she was referring to when she demanded a correct understanding of her place in history. Her painful path to revelation, discovery, and proof.

> Every statement in "Science and Health" I have gained through suffering. Every step of advancement at my home of my own and . . . of the students is reached in the same "strait and narrow" way.[4]

Her life is a testament to cross-bearing, even before she returned from the South as a widow and lived the next years from pillar to post, unable to be with her own child, many times scorned and rejected as she moved on to learn the source of Christian healing. Those in the household knew that; she sometimes spoke of it in veiled and not-so-veiled ways.

Was this dignifying a human past or making a reality of "error"? On the contrary, she had come to feel that Christian Scientists were in danger of becoming complacent, comfortable, as ease claimed them. There is no ease in matter, she maintained. Also involved was the progressive understanding she had of sin as the real culprit in mortal existence. The healing of sin had become predominant in her thinking even over the healing of disease; in fact, she had found that disease cannot be healed if sin remains in thought.

As long as sins were allowed to remain in thinking, they needed to be destroyed—with the process being self-destruction of this unreal component of life. She was quick to point out sin on the part of the household staff; she recognized error as coming in both blatant and subtle forms. Dickey said that not everyone could stand this constant scrutiny and correction, but he had determined "to be obedient in every case," as he wrote in his *Memoirs*. He took her at her word that the suffering that had come to her was always related to the advancement of the cause. Thus had it always been; thus it continued even in these later days.

His *Memoirs* reports that Mrs. Eddy asked him to take pencil and paper and write what she dictated. It was this:

> I prayed God day and night to show me how to form my Church, and how to go on with it. I understand that He showed me, just as I understand He showed me Christian Science, and no human being ever showed me Christian Science. Then I have no right or desire to change what God has directed me to do, and it remains for the Church to obey it. What has prospered this Church for thirty years will continue to keep it.

On another occasion she said with some degree of anguish, "What is to become of this Cause? . . . .. If error can do this to me [her suffering] what is it going to do to you?"

Dickey describes the physical anguish that occurred when she was contemplating some change in the structure of a by-law or change in Church management:

> The needs of her Church were frequently met through the enactment of some By-law, which, though it startled the Christian Science field, yet it seemed to be the imperative demand of

Wisdom made upon our leader. At times these decisions were arrived at after long nights of prayer and struggle.

It was not a view that the "sweetness-and-light" congregations far away from Boston understood. She wished they did because only when they picked up the burden of sorrow and worked their way through it to Christ-like selfhood, would their demonstration of Christian oneness with God be demonstrated.

She had known personally of what she wrote when she said in *Science and Health* [p. 48:10-14]:

> Remembering the sweat of agony which fell in holy bene-diction on the grass of Gethsemane, shall the humblest or might-iest disciple murmur when he drinks from the same cup, and think, or even wish, to escape the exalting ordeal of sin's revenge on its destroyer?

But she did promise the crown along with the cross in this statement from the same passage: "Truth and Love bestow few palms until the consummation of a life-work." Thousands of adherents of the Truth were waving false palms out there somewhere. She knew all too well that those palms would probably be trampled underfoot the next week.

Her views about suffering were frequently shared with Dickey. In a household note sent to him in July of 1909 she said:

> Mr. Dickey C.S.B.
>
> Beloved in God
> I thank you for taking up the cross and following Christ.
> We cannot follow Him in any other way.
>
> > Lovingly yours
> > Mary Baker Eddy[5]

Robert Peel describes the Adam Dickey of this time as being "built like a blacksmith or a prizefighter, endowed with no conspicuous graces of mind or manner."[6] But "Mr. Dickey" had the graces that Mrs. Eddy needed: an unshakable faith in God, an unquestioning trust in her leadership, and an unswerving determination to serve the cause she led. And he knew she had willingly accepted the burden of suffering so that the cause might advance.

Advance it did. Many were the changes and polishings for the Christian Science movement that flew from her thought and the pen of her aman-uensis during these months of 1908.

These steps were often accomplished in the face of attacks, both mental and physical. When Mrs. Eddy was still at Pleasant View, she had been in such pain that eventually those around her believed a diagnosis was in order. A physician came and pronounced kidney stones, a malady that produces challenging pain. Other physicians came in from time to time and confirmed the diagnosis and administered morphine, the only painkiller of the day, at her request.

In June of 1908 Mrs Eddy experienced what Dickey described as "an attack of unusual severity." At the time, thousands of the faithful poured into Boston for the gathering at Communion Season. She believed they were directing adulating, worshipful thought at her, and it was causing the difficulty. She called for Dickey, and he took down a by-law abolishing the Communion Season at The Mother Church, effective the following year. Immediately she rose and went to her desk and began work, freed from her pain.

It was a startling decision. Christian Scientists looked forward to combining social and spiritual interests by coming to The Mother Church just before its annual meeting for communion. Mrs. Eddy's answer was that they could still commune spiritually with God wherever they were, and it would be far better for them to do that than to just look forward to greeting each other and wallowing in human religious ecstasy in the grand, if not grandiose, Extension of The Mother Church. But some said that many of the Christian Scientists now in town had come out of the Protestant tradition of sacred ceremony for the time of communion, and they invested their annual time at The Mother Church with this fervor. So, to say the least, not everyone approved of her move. On this occasion Adelaide Still, Mrs. Eddy's personal maid, reported that Calvin Frye said to her, "She'll ruin her Church."

Adam Dickey describes himself as obedient to his leader's decrees, and that summer he had occasion to prove that he generally was in accord with her. Mrs. Eddy, probably reinforced in her intent by a letter from a thoughtful student who was also a veteran journalist, had decided to found a newspaper. *The Christian Science Monitor* was in its early stages of development. She had waited until the Publishing Society building was completed next to The Mother Church, then had written to the directors that she wanted to implement right away the project to establish the newspaper. The original notes Dickey used for his memoir, done week by week, record for a date in this period that Mrs Eddy intended to found a newspaper. He supported it. But Frye did not. He said they all had enough trouble around Chestnut Hill without that.

Dickey did oppose his leader, sometimes strongly, when he believed he needed to. On July 2, according to Frye's diary, Mrs. Eddy wrote to Frye:

Beloved

If you knew with what I am beset continually arguments of dementia incompetence old age etc. it would explain why I am so changed.

Mr. Dickey yields to M.A.M. to such an extent he affords me very little help in anything. I have to correct him continually.[8]

Others were strongly reprimanded from time to time during this year; Mrs. Eddy believed in speaking the word in season to error. William R. Rathvon, a Colorado Christian Scientist, came to assist Dickey late in the year. Another Kimball student, he was of the breed of practiced and confident Christian Scientists who had replaced almost all of the rough-hewn and spontaneous pioneers—except Frye. He, too, felt the sting of her rebuke.

The founder did not stop for any reason in guiding her church forward. Increasingly insisting that the directors turn to the *Manual* and their own prayerful intuition, she carefully edited the *Manual* during 1908 and 1909. The important by-law forbidding interference by any church (even The Mother Church) in a branch church's affairs strengthened the democratic basis of branch church work.

The fact that Mrs. Eddy was an octogenarian did not dissuade the haters around the world, who increased their attacks. Who could tell the real story? She received word in the summer of 1908 that journalist Sibyl Wilbur was about to release a fulsome and shallow biography

She asked Wilbur to hold the release. Discussing the matter with Mrs. Eddy, Dickey wondered if they should not allow some kind of favorable biography to be put out, since Milmine's caustic *Life of Mary Baker Eddy*, based on the *McClure's Magazine* series, was being readied for publication. She acceded, reluctantly, and Wilbur's biography appeared.

If her biography was to be written, Mrs. Eddy apparently wanted it to be a deep and searching story of her spiritual road and dimensions. She wanted to have the elements of suffering for Christ and the effects on the mind and body of the world's actively directed hostility, so she called her chief secretary in to her apartment on Tuesday, August 26, 1908, and extracted a promise from him. He describes it this way:

Requesting Mrs. Sargent, Mr. Frye, and a third student to leave the room, she beckoned me to approach. She extended her hand to me, took mine in both of hers, and asked in a deep, earnest voice, "Mr. Dickey, I want you to promise me something, will you?"

I said, "Yes, Mother, I certainly will."

"Well," she continued, "if I should ever leave here—do you

know what I mean by that?"

"Yes, Mother."

"If I should ever leave here," she repeated, "will you promise me that you will write a history of what has transpired in your
experiences with me, and say that I was mentally murdered?"

I answered. "Yes, Mother, I will."

"Now, Mr. Dickey, do not let anything interfere with your
keeping this promise. Will you swear to me before God that you
will not fail to carry out my wish?"

I raised my right hand and said, "Mother, I swear before
God that I will do what you request of me, namely, write a history of what I have seen, and heard from your lips concerning
your life."

"That will do, dear. I know now that you will not fail me."

He was trying hard not to fail her.

By December of 1908, Dickey missed Lillian so much that he believed
he could no longer stay at Chestnut Hill. The William Rathvon diary entry
for December 27, 1908, states that in a conversation with "AD" Dickey con-
fided that Lillian also was so unhappy with the "present arrangement" that
she believed the couple might have to separate. But Dickey would leave Mrs.
Eddy before allowing that to occur.

The Dickeys were only two of many for whom the rigid schedule of
Chestnut Hill became too much. Rathvon explains that Mrs. Eddy seldom
had vacations or outings in her own life, thus, she expected those in her
household to stay with her day and night without relief. The cause demanded unstinting effort, and she needed them. Rathvon's own marital situation
was relieved when his wife Ella came to the household, and eventually Mrs.
Eddy allowed Lillian Dickey to come to Boston and visit Chestnut Hill from
time to time. She also relented on the practice of no outings or outside visi-
tations in the case of the Dickeys, and Adam visited his wife at her lodgings,
a situation which was satisfactory for them at least for the moment.

It was mark of favor for him, indicating the amount of affection the
leader felt for this man who had become like a son to her. The special treatment caused comments among the staff, especially Frye, who believed she
was showing favoritism.

Rathvon in his December 28 diary entry praises Dickey for his loyalty.
He writes that he feels drawn to him because, like himself, Dickey believed
Mrs. Eddy was ordained to give *Science and Health* to the world. That Dickey
was close-mouthed about the business he was transacting had good and
bad sides. No gossip leaked out until official steps were taken, but the staff
at Chestnut Hill might benefit from more information. Rathvon does not
hesitate to delineate what he sees as Dickey's faults:

He stands staunchly by all those whom he likes, and is correspondingly indifferent to the affairs of those who please him not, and thereby prejudges the motives of all classes or individuals who have, with or without cause, gained his disapproval. This accounts for much of the friction between him and CF [Calvin Frye].

With more flexibility, breadth of vision and tolerance he will be more effective to the Cause, and these things he is endeavoring to cultivate. He is a faithful student of the books, and has done good work as a practitioner.[9]

Chapter Seven

Faithful to the End

If Mary Baker Eddy emphasized to her students the bearing of the cross, self-sacrifice, and humility to attain the crown of life in Spirit, Augusta Stetson, an ostentatious Christian Science teacher in New York City, was not listening. Her New York branch for many years had exhibited a streak of rebellion, materialism, and flamboyance.

When Stetson announced plans in New York papers for building a "branch" of her First Church to make it appear to rival The Mother Church, Mrs. Eddy had to act. Calling her long-time student and friend to Boston, she went on a drive with her and allowed her to withdraw her plans. She would not see Augusta Stetson again, but it could not have been easy to sever a twenty-five-year relationship.

When Mrs. Stetson continued to implement her baroque control of New York churches and to show signs of instability, Mrs. Eddy wrote her a letter that implied she should not contact her further ". . . Mr. Adam Dickey is my secretary, through whom all my business is transacted."[1]

As the final, dreary act of the Stetson drama wore on, Dickey found Mrs. Eddy seeking his advice on this most threatening issue she was facing. She could not bear to let Stetson go. Perhaps she should be reinstated to The Mother Church. Their association had been so long, and the head of the New York church had done such spectacular work in the past. Rathvon reported that on his night "watch" Dickey had told Mrs. Eddy that she would lose the church if Stetson were reinstated. She listened, and the next morning seemed fresher and by Christmas, ten days later, was lively and actively at work.[2]

Dickey was not the grand vizier of the household, though claims at that time and later would imply this. During this period he had convinced Mrs. Eddy that his wife Lillian would be a useful addition to the household staff, and Mrs. Dickey took up residence and began working as part of the team. But two Dickeys were just too much, and staff members told Mrs. Eddy that having Lillian there added to the dissention among her "family."

The leader was still the leader, and she told Lillian that she was not needed as a staff person and that she should return to her status as a sometime visitor, whereupon Dickey reportedly had a confrontation with Calvin Frye.[3]

The founder of Christian Science was moving to stabilize and depersonalize the movement. She would not be on earth forever and the "succession," she maintained stoutly, was not to be a person, either male or female, but the spiritual man. She instructed Dickey to send to Archibald McLellan for the *Christian Science Sentinel* of January 15, 1910, a notice that encouraged deep rooting of democracy in branch churches.

> She believes that all branch churches that have been controlled by any one teacher, or the students of any one teacher, will find it greatly to their advantage to change to a broader and more liberal form of government.[4]

A right concept of organization was the need of the day, Mrs. Eddy insisted, telling Judge Smith, "Christian Scientists who go about saying that we need no organization are not knowing what they are talking about." Organization would prevail when she died, and she must have realized that that time could not be far off.

Dickey found himself pitted against the men who were long-recognized administrators of the church, as the question of church organization and the succession came to the forefront in the last year of her life. After all, the *Manual* stated that no business could be transacted without her explicit signature. How could that be obtained if she was not present? The whole structure seemed in danger of being petrified at the time of her passing.

Rathvon consulted with Judges Septimus J. Hanna and Clifford P. Smith, who spoke to Dickey about an advisory board supposedly representing Mrs. Eddy's interest. This board would speak on her behalf if she could not. He asked Dickey to present the plan to Mrs. Eddy, but Dickey refused. There was no need for this stratagem, he insisted. Although Mrs. Eddy was asking to be relieved of responsibilities, she was not incompetent. "You made a mistake in taking this matter to Judge Smith and Judge Hanna," he told them.[5] He supported Mrs. Eddy's radical stand about changes in church law: only from God, not from the wishes of men. "God has taken care of our cause thus far, and He will not desert it now," Dickey told Rathvon, who could hardly disagree.

In the midst of the issues of controversy and church building, there was time sometimes for reflection and even fun. Dickey records occasions when the group gathered to sing old hymns, and gatherings when, chuckling, Mrs. Eddy told old stories about her father's Irish help. Often her mouth would show a wry smile when something amused her.

And the family joined in prayer, though not always with her present.

Interestingly, Mrs. Eddy at this time instituted a practice that had not been common in the Christian Science church. She asked the group gathered around her for devotions to offer audible prayers. Perhaps she did this to test individual metaphysics; and the group did the best they could at these times. In the Dickey collection at the Mary Baker Eddy Library is a prayer by him, as it was typed on what seems to be his own typewriter.

> Prayer
> We thank Thee O Divine Love for the joy that is ours, in knowing that we are the children and the offspring of infinite Mind. We thank Thee for the wonderful discovery of Christian Science, that reveals to us the nature of our divine inheritance, and show us the barrenness and nothingness of human sense.
>
> We thank Thee that in all this world there was one whose spiritual vision was clear enough to pierce the darkness of mortal mind and disclose to a waiting world a true knowledge of God.
>
> We thank Thee dear Father that ours is the joy and the privilege of not only living in the same age and in the same country, but that we are in the same house and in the very presence of the one whom thou hast chosen to receive this wonderful revelation and give it to mankind.
>
> May our appreciation of this blessed privilege be manifested in our daily lives. May we be better men and women, better Christians, better healers and teachers, always ready to support the work whenever and wherever called up.[6]
> Amen

As 1909 spun out, difficulties seemed to pass and problems be solved; even the quandary of son George Glover's feared attempt to break Mrs. Eddy's will was settled by November, 1909.[7] He agreed to a settlement that involved both cash and funds in trust in return for renouncing future claims on his mother's estate. A post-mortem attempt by the son later failed.

The kidney stone complaint, however, seemed to reach climaxes at night in early 1910, and the leader asked the physician to give her morphine to ease her pain. Finally, on May 9, Frye says Dickey told her they were not going to allow more morphine; she did not need it since stones seemed to have passed. It was the "old morphine habit" reasserting itself, and he would not let her have it.

Dickey saw that his leader in the throes of pain had called for the physician to relieve her enough in the past few years to make it a potential habit, and he realized that it was not necessary since symptoms were abating.

She grew more frail and detached by the summer of 1910. Many evenings were quiet, the malicious animal magnetism squad not called for. Many days Mrs. Eddy stayed alone in her room with her maid. Most of her affairs passed into Dickey's hands: periodical articles, letters, and appointments. He did take two weeks off to return to Kansas City to finally settle a lawsuit arising from his practice—Welsh Vs. Dickey—but returned as soon as possible. Letters came asking what specifics to teach in Sunday School, what Mrs Eddy's views were on this and that, how to react to political issues. Dickey answered them all, taking some of the more important to her.

Dickey became the *de facto* voice of Mary Baker Eddy. Years later he was praised for having stayed true to her vision. Her uncompromising insistence—born of absolute conviction and years of experience—that God, the divine Mind who is Love, would meet every human need—was equally his own. If the cross of suffering had marked her life in a way it had not marked his, it did not matter. They shared the crown of demonstration and confidence in the allness of God.

In November of 1910, she "caught cold," and her strength seemed to ebb daily. She still insisted, in an understandably crochety way, that she go out in her carriage. Laura was at her side during the rides, but they were an effort.

December 4 a notice was read at The Mother Church service that Mary Baker Eddy had passed from this earth on December 3. Laura Sargent and Dickey had been at her side.

Interestingly, a little more than a year before, Dickey had written for Mrs. Eddy a reply to a letter dated October 25, 1909. It was from a fellow student of Edward Kimball, who had recently died. This inquirer wondered about activity beyond this earth:

> I am not at liberty to quote our leader verbatim, but my sense of the points you enquire about after talking with her on the subject is that. . .
>
> Thought on the other side of the grave is not different from thought on this side. Edward Kimball is not dead and has not stopped his C.S. work. In fact he knows he has not died and he still teaches and holds association meetings. Good may therefore flow from him to his students through the efficacy of enlightened thought.[8]

In light of this letter, one may wonder if Dickey thought Mrs. Eddy, too, might still be teaching and having her own associations out of human sight.

A few duties remained for him in the Chestnut Hill house. Assisting officials like Archibald McLellan and Alfred Farlow, he and others on the staff prepared for the "viewing" of Mary Baker Eddy in the downstairs parlor and for her burial in Mount Auburn Cemetery in Cambridge.

Dickey had turned out to be the man of the hour for the Christian Science movement in the last years of her life. His service was a matter of both style and substance. Dickey was the practical, even-tempered, but well schooled and experienced student of Christian Science.

But even more importantly, Dickey practiced Christian Science in the mode of the movement's founder. Mrs. Eddy's religious style in the day-to-day life has not been often analyzed, but it is obvious from her writings during the time she was at Pleasant View and Chestnut Hill. She was a prag-matic practitioner of Christian Science, a walk-the-road, follow-the-Master Christian.

In the 1860s and early 70s, she had been more speculative. A look at her exegesis of the book of Genesis in *In My True Light: Collections from the Mary Baker Eddy Library for the Betterment of Humanity* shows her attempting to put Biblical language into her own spiritual "tongue," concerned about the deepest ontological meanings of her discovery. By the 1890s she was concentrating on the results of practicing the Science of Christianity in daily life. She saw proving of her Science as a practicum, an internship in the cur-riculum of "earth's preparatory school." No one would understand this Sci-ence, be attracted to it, or stick with it, unless he or she could see results.

> Though demonstrating his control over sin and disease, the great Teacher by no means relieved others from giving the requisite proofs of their own piety. He worked for their guid-ance, that they might demonstrate this power as he did and un-derstand its divine Principle. Implicit faith in the Teacher and all the emotional love we can bestow on him, will never alone make us imitators of him. We must go and do likewise, else we are not improving the great blessings which our Master worked and suffered to bestow on us. [S&H, p. 25:22-31]

Decades of Bible study and her own personal experience turned her ever more deeply to the teachings of Jesus. She saw the spirit that animated him as the eternal Christ, Truth, coming to the human experience every-where, establishing the true view of man. This could be realized in everyday experience. Salvation was the intersection of the timeless Christ with the human experience, exalting it, healing it, raising it into consciousness of the Son of God. And demonstrating that Christ, which based its power on the Allness of God and no other power, was each person's daily task: to wit, progressively casting out sin, sickness, and the belief in death.

And she warned of the crown of thorns that was part of practicing Christianity as science: "The trials encountered by prophet, disciple, and apostle, 'of whom the world was not worthy,' await in some form, every pioneer of truth." [S&H, p. 25:28-29]

So many letters she wrote, almost every communication to her church in the last decade of her life, were calls for walking the healing walk along the roads of life, whether they were to Bethany, Emmaus, or Back Bay.

Some took her teaching into abstraction, but Mrs. Eddy did not speak often in theoretical terms at this period. She worked to live according to the absolute, but her practice was demonstrative Christian Science.

The class notes of some teachers of the period, some of which were presumably preserved against their instructions, show that a degree of teaching focused strongly on the purely ontological aspects of Mrs. Eddy's teaching, the "being" rather than the "walking." But it is not the emphasis she placed on what should be happening in her movement in her latter days. Dickey was the same sort of hands-on practitioner: base each day's experience on perfect God and perfect man as the basis of thought and demonstration, and go out and follow Jesus in the marketplace—in his case originally in the clay pipe factory, later in the offices of The Mother Church Board of Directors.

Mrs. Eddy never condoned poor behavior—the many forms of sin that denied the perfect man of God's creating. Her students who cringed at her strong rebukes did not understand that she was rebuking the sin in their thinking, helping them establish the perfect model, concentrating on the "Christianization of daily life." It was her way, arrived at through years of advanced learning: and Dickey was in that way a person of similar thought about Christian behavior when she needed one.

So Mrs. Eddy helped him to favor in the movement, and her partiality followed him the remainder of his life. She had his portrait hung at Chestnut Hill next to her own and that of her beloved husband, Gilbert Eddy. She had autographed the first copy of *Poems*, which she had authorized him to organize and publish. When he showed her the copy of the book, she called it "beautiful."

The arranging and publication of the poems was only one of the accomplishments Dickey had to his credit during the years with her. Longyear Historical Society's Anne Holiday Webb recounted his accomplishment with the German edition of *Science and Health*:

> When a request for a German translation of Science and Health with Key to the Scriptures was approved by Mrs. Eddy, she directed Mr. Dickey to oversee this work. Miss Florence M. Dickey of Kansas city, Adam Dickey's sister, has left this record of the initial steps in this work: "When the committee appointed by The Christian Science Board of Directors of The Mother Church met to translate the textbook . . . from English into Ger-

man, the first day of their meeting Mr. Archibald McLellan told them that Mrs. Eddy had instructed Mr. Dickey to watch the translation and to guard the metaphysical meaning of each line.[9] This he did scrupulously.

The German Translation of *Science and Health*

A document in the Mary Baker Eddy Library written by Ulla Schultz Oldenburg shows the meticulous but creative process involved in translating *Science and Health* into German.

Frau Oldenburg details the organization of the task: three fluent English speakers were recruited in Germany to separately translate the textbook into German. After the completion they were to meet in Boston to compare their versions, coming up with a final translation. Renata Hermes (later King) and Graf Helmuth von Moltke joined Ulla Schultz on the translating team. Oldenburg says:

"Adam H. Dickey had been asked by our leader to watch the translation, as Mr. McLellan [Archibald McLellan of the Board of Directors] informed us the day of our arrival. Grafin Dorothee von Moltke being English was elected in order to literally translate our translations back to Mr. Dickey, paragraph by paragraph, for him to consider especially whether the committee had given the metaphysics right. . . .The German Christian Scientists' gratitude to our leader for her precious gift of the translation is inseparably bound up with unceasing gratitude to Adam H. Dickey for the stupendous work he did during all those months of the translation. Only his great love for our leader, for her textbook and his dutiful care to carry out her wish could have enabled him to self-sacrificingly 'watch' in never ceasing patience and encouraging love. Indeed, his works do follow him."

SF Box 108 Courtesy Mary Baker Eddy collection

Later his German friends sent letters of appreciation, which he answered. A letter of May 27, 1913, replies to a question about attacks on Christian Science:

You speak of the claim of discord that is at work in Ger-

many, but I think you will find that wherever Christian Science
is advancing rapidly, these symptoms of dissatisfaction usually accompany it. The belief is not confined to any particular locality.
It is a universal claim and belongs to neither person, place nor
thing. The only way, as you know, is to hold firmly in thought
the right idea of God and His creation, and the discordant sense
of things will be unable to find the place in our thought. This is
what we call rising above error.[10]

Dickey held the degree C.S.D., conferred on him for his individual
teaching by Mrs. Eddy and his contribution to her work. But as he left
Chestnut Hill, not everyone was sorry to see him go. Excerpts from the Frye
diary reflect the conflicts between the two.

Mr. Dickey and Mr. Frye:
Highlights from the Calvin Frye diary

2/5/08: Mr. Adam H. Dickey came to act as secretary today.

3/15/08: Mrs. Eddy took her first ride in automobile today. Mrs. Sargent Mrs. Tomlinson and M[r] Rathvon rode inside
with her[.] She was followed by Mr Dickey driving her carriage.

7/27/08: Mrs. Eddy told me today that The Mother
Church offered to pay A.H. Dickey $2500 per year.

9/24/08: Mrs. Eddy looked at Sybil [sic] Wilbur's book
today and told Mr. A. H. Dickey that they might go ahead with
publishing it.

3/25/09: Mrs. Eddy raised Mr. Dickey's salary from $1300
to $1500 today.

5/16/09: Mrs. Eddy called her students to her room this
afternoon to tell us, "We have all in God, and God is all and she
added [`]This realized is the blessing of blessings!!"

7/29/09: Mrs. Eddy told me this morning to pay Mr Dickey $1000 more per year than the others because he does more
than the others. And to have this increase of wages date from
now. But he declined to change his salary.

8/28/09: Mr. Walter Dickey was in Boston today and
Adam H. was visiting him there for about 2 hours.

9/11/09: Mrs. Eddy told M.A. Still [i.e., Adelaide Still]
that [she?] shall have the same wages as mental workers. She also

told me that A.H. Dickey and I are to have hereafter $5,000 each per year.

9/22/09: Mrs. Eddy received Gen. H.M. Baker's resignation as her trustee today and today appointed Adam H. Dickey as his successor.

12/21/09: Mrs. Eddy granted A. H. Dickey 2 weeks off to go to Kansas City today.

1/12/10: Mr Adam H. Dickey brought his wife to Mrs. Eddy's home this afternoon to stay.

1/14/10: Mrs. Eddy called her watchers to her this morning and told us she did not invite Mrs Dickey to come here to stay but upon Mr Dickey's insistence she consented to let her come & visit him.

1/22/10: Mr. AH Dickey was down to Beaconsfield Hotel today from 7.30 to 6 p.m.

3/20/10: A.H. Dickey had a day off today & took an automobile ride to Gloucester with his wife.

4/9/10: Mrs. A.H. Dickey had an interview with Mrs. Eddy today and dined with the family.

5/9/10: [Well known references to Mrs. Eddy and no more morphine declared by AHD.] "Mr. Adam H. Dickey last night told Mrs. Eddy that she shall not have any more morphine."

5/27/10: Mrs. A.H. Dickey was at C.H. Home today to dinner and intends to stay a while.

6/27/10: Mrs. Adam H. Dickey returned from Kansas City and came today to live at Mrs. Eddy's home.

7/2/10: I asked Mrs. Eddy this evening if she intended to have Mrs. A.H. Dickey be one of her mental workers and she replied "No, I never thought of such a thing."

7/10/10: Mrs. Eddy called me to her room today and told me not to pay Mrs. AH Dickey for services but let her remain with Mr. Dickey free of expense.

7/18/10: Mrs. Eddy called her assistants to her room today several times & talked about whether it is right for her to keep so many there when they did not seem to give her the help she needs & could do so much more good elsewhere: she decided to let Mrs. Rathvon and Mrs. Dickey go away.

7/21/10: Mrs. A. H. Dickey returned to live at her hotel this afternoon.

7/23/10: Mrs. A. H. Dickey came to live at Mrs. Eddy's home again this afternoon.

7/28/10: Mr. Adam H. Dickey accused me [Frye] today of preventing his wife from remaining in Mrs. Eddy's home. Afterwards, this evening Mrs. Eddy called Mrs. Dickey to her room and asked her about her old beliefs and Mrs. Dickey admitted that about twenty years ago she was healed of sciatica nerve.

7/29/10: Mrs. Adam H. Dickey returned to Hotel Beaconsfield again today.

8/1/10: Mr. Dickey got Mrs. Eddy's consent to go to Boston this p.m. to visit his students.

8/21/10: She [Mrs. Eddy] watched from her windows last even. Mr. Dickey and Mr. and Mrs. Rathvon toss ball and D[ickey]trying to walk on his hands, and the result was a very disturbed night and fear she could not live! [Note: the William Rathvon diary references these events on the lawn at Chestnut Hill, but tells what a success they were. The difference in opinion is striking.]

10/3/10: Geo H. Kinter arrived at C. Hill to remain while A.H. Dickey goes to Kansas City to attend law suit case of Welch vs. Dickey.

11/21/10: Adam H. Dickey was today elected a member of the Christian Science Board of Directors of the Mother Church Boston by request of Mrs. Eddy.

12/4/10: Our beloved leader, the Rev. Mary Baker G. Eddy, "entered into her rest" last night at 10:45 quietly without a struggle.

5/11/11: Was over at Chestnut Hill today to pay bills&c, Gen Baker came there with Streeter and A.Farlow and Adam Dickey & wife called. Question: where was Mrs. Eddy's legal residence?[11]

The leader was gone, so it did not matter what Frye thought. Adam Dickey had packed his trunk and valise, including mementos and notes on his stay and left the mansion that had been his home almost every day for two years. He and Lillian would be living in the Boston area permanently, since Mrs. Eddy's last official act had been to appoint him to the board of directors.

Adam Dickey driving the "family car" with Lillian in front and William Rathvon, Laura E. Sargent, and Ella S. Rathvon in the rear seat. The Chesnut
Hill mansion stands in the background. Mrs. Eddy liked keeping up with new
technologies. The notes at the end of the Chesnut Hill Album in the second
part of this book show her agreeing to have her voice recorded. There is no
account remaining that shows this was ever done. What a treasure that would
have been for her admirers and followers! Perhaps a recording of Mrs. Eddy's
voice will surface some day. The leader also inquired about, and was interested
in, the recent first flights of airplanes.

The household dining room at Chestnut Hill while Mr. Dickey was there. Calvin Frye is in the foreground, Dickey to the left of him and William Rathvon to the left of Dickey.

Courtesy Keith McNeil Collection

Adam Dickey's personal collection of photos of Mrs. Eddy includes this famous one of her on the balcony at Pleasant View, Communion Season, 1903. *Courtesy Mary Baker Eddy Library.*

Mrs. Eddy with the special diamond cross, from Dickey's own collection. *Courtesy Mary Baker Eddy Library.*

Chapter Eight

Under Scrutiny with Board Duties

Adam Dickey served on The Christian Science Board of Directors with Ira O.Knapp, Stephen A. Chase, Archibald McLellan, and John V. Dittemore.[1] All hoped the forward motion of the movement Mary Baker Eddy had established would continue without interruption and that the church would continue to grow. So did its adherents around the world.

The board members recognized no other way of achieving that than to take up the reins themselves. Dickey knew Mrs. Eddy intended the board to function and move on. She had specified management duties for them in the *Manual*: maintenance of the lectureship function, the committees on publication and many other responsibilities. She had already turned over matters to the board for several years; they were an accomplished "fact."

Many in the general public believed the movement would not continue. But the board met as often as necessary during a week to pray the Daily Prayer Mrs. Eddy had taught her followers, read minutes of former meetings, and perform their duties, showing tangibly the continuity of the church. Challenges to the very church structure appeared immediately, and intensified during the decade. For example, some felt the by-laws could not stand as articulated in the *Manual* because of its provision:

> No new Tenet or By-law shall be adopted, nor any Tenet or
> By-law amended or annulled, without the written consent of Mary
> Baker Eddy, the author of our textbook *Science and Health*.

The board decided to take Mrs. Eddy's name off the Listing of Church Officers published in the *Manual* in 1911. This title had been bestowed upon her by the board, and it followed that it was in their jurisdiction to remove it. Rumors circulating around Boston contributed to their decision; some people were saying that the board had kept her name among the officers because they believed she would be resurrected. They could not have that rumor continue, and they needed to act to be sure the by-laws of the

Manual stood, ready to serve the future.

Another faction of Mother Church members felt that the membership, acting as a body, represented the governing authority of the church. The board was not legitimate. Still, the fact that the board functioned was a statement in itself. Possession and day-to-day showing up at the office were nine tenths of the law.

In a cabinet-style government, each director had responsibility for a major supervisory area. Dickey became Treasurer in 1912 and continued in that position until 1917. His business experience was valued as appeals for funds went out to the field and management of the properties and general accounting made many demands. The publications needed to be supervised, and their personnel and financial accounts overseen.

These were immediate concerns. But long-range duties also emerged, falling into two general categories: extending the movement's reach and protecting it from attack. These would be directions as long as Dickey was on the board.

As far as the first concern went, Christian Scientists in the villages where their churches and societies functioned were extending the religion essentially on their own. Their enthusiasm and healing testified to what Science could do. Publicity was often good. The *Christian Science Sentinel* printed remarkable testimonies, and copies of the periodical were put in public places and shared with friends.

A few had particular impact. For example, after the *Titanic* sank, one of its stewards gave a memorable testimony in the October, 1912, *Journal*, about the power of God to save and heal. He was sucked down with the boat, but as he realized the power of God, was thrust to the surface more than once and survived the frigid water for hours until rescue.

Individuals were being drawn in, one by one, intrigued by what neighbors reported. In Indianapolis in the author's family, a twelve-year-old girl stood at the back of the parlor of her home and listened to a couple from down the street talk about this healing form of Christianity—and presented to the family a book they said had helped them immeasurably. The girl was the one who took up the book and today, with ninety-seven years to her credit, she is still a devoted student of Christian Science. The "parlor presentations" happened all across America.

Renaissance-style temples, handsome colonial chapels and simple wooden and stone churches with Sunday Schools in their basements began to dot the city and town landscapes of America, with "First Church of Christ, Scientist" (or "Second" or even "Sixth") above their portals. During 1912 sixty-five churches and societies were organized in the United States, Canada, Europe, South America, Australia and New Zealand. Translations of *Science and Health* had to be supervised from Boston; new congregations overseen. There were over 5,000 practitioners world-wide; their concerns

had to be met. There was also general institutional growth to plan and implement.

Everybody was interested in what that would be. Factions buzzed, seizing on every bit of sweet gossip and news from "church headquarters." Practitioners in Georgia and Maine talked about what "Mr. Dickey" and the
other board members promulgated. Almost everybody had an opinion on
how things "ought to be run." It could not have been easy for the men in
the church offices. Decisions that had to be made to move the institutional
machinery forward were done in the midst of students' yapping and baying
about their heels.

What to do with the Pleasant View house was only one of the questions to be settled, and this topic would be the subject of discussion during
the next ten years, along with the issue of the other properties Mrs. Eddy
had owned. Gradually the house decayed until the board had to tear it
down, and eventually the site became a home for Christian Science practitioners and nurses of advanced years. Fortunately, eventually a wealthy
student, Mary Beecher Longyear, took up the cause of some of the other
historical buildings.

Also significant was the proposition of a Christian Science "hospital," which became a major focus for the board and particularly for Adam
Dickey, who had several times discussed it with Mrs. Eddy.

He contended that the establishment of a "sanatorium" under the care
of the already existing Christian Science Benevolent Association was in "direct obedience to our leader's wishes."[2] She had even set up a by-law in 1909
calling for a care facility, which she repealed because the board complained
it did not have time to supervise it.

A 1916 article entitled "A Progressive Step," which crystallized discussions in the board and across the movement of some five years, spelled out
Mrs. Eddy's wishes for practical care for the sick:

> Our leader was for many years deeply impressed with the
> thought that the Christian Science movement should have places
> where people suffering from ills of various sorts could retire for
> treatment, rest and recuperation. The members of Mrs. Eddy's
> household who ministered to her needs have heard her many
> times express herself quite freely on this subject. She knew that
> many times patients under Christian Science treatment were at
> times placed in a position where they needed the care and atten-
> tion of a skillfully trained person who was also a Christian Scien-
> tist. . . . as well as freedom from criticism while under Christian
> Science treatment.

The passage also reveals a writing style that would become familiar to readers in the movement as the "Dickey style," characterized by:

(1) A direct tone that reached for authority right back to Mary Baker Eddy. Dickey utilized his close, personal association to strengthen his and the board's directives. It was difficult to refute this sort of "I-heard-her-say this-when-I-was-there" approach, but it was irritating to others, particularly co-pioneers in the movement during Mrs. Eddy's last days. Rathvon, who it will be remembered had been in the household with Dickey and was not his strongest supporter, was reputed to have been incensed when Dickey used her authority to prove some point.

(2) Rock-bottom, simple metaphysics that are easy to understand. "God is all there is, and when you have said that, you have said all there is to say." This lack of subtle abstraction was to cause him enemies as board years wore on.

(3) An ultra-sensitive consciousness of what the press would say about each and every thing that the Christian Science movement would do. This he and the others had learned in the school of hard knocks.

The paragraph in the 1916 *Sentinel* article explains much in terms of board awareness as to what newspapers might say about Christian Scientists:

> It is quite likely that newspaper men will express their views of this new activity of our cause, hence the advisability of Scientists refraining from making statements in advance of their present demonstration. The metaphysical fact is that all is Mind and Mind's ideas, that there is nothing in this universe but Mind and what Mind creates. The real newspaper, then, the avenue or the channel through which authentic information is given out, can be nothing more or less than the voice of Truth—of wisdom uttering itself and declaring itself to human consciousness

In this case Dickey was referring to the idea that now that Christian Scientists were going to have "hospitals" (as he called them) they might also eventually have "schools, orphans homes and insane asylums." He entertained that possibility for the future. These things were not finally established "from Boston," not at least in the case of schools established by Christian Scientists in the field.

But why were Scientists talking about "hospitals" and insane asylums some students wanted to know? The establishment of care institutions would only cement the common feeling that illness was a reality, wouldn't it? The sanatoria might foster talk about disease or nurture a focus on the details of various illnesses, as nurses bustled about, writing charts, discussing cases.

Dickey and his associates, however, believed that common humanity should dictate that people "laboring under a belief" should be afforded care.

And, he insisted, Mrs. Eddy wanted it.

The second great long-term task was the defense against enemies. First, at least for Dickey, was the protection of the leader's reputation. *McClure's Magazine* and Mark Twain had already presented a dreadful picture of her. In 1907 Reverend Lyman Powell had published a book that relied on false information in earlier articles and dug up even more disenchanted friends and relatives to show her as grasping, dissembling, and sometimes hysterical. Now, as Mrs. Eddy's name passed into history, periodicals of the day summed up her career. While some praised her work as throwing fresh light on Christianity, other articles continued the abusive pattern.

Allowing false pictures to continue in the public mind threatened the growth of the cause. Dickey was particularly interested in the *Manual*-directed work of the one-man committees on publication, which functioned as corrective agencies in communities where the movement was established.

Both in a capacity as board contact of the committees on publication and as a board member, he enjoyed speaking to the "committees" who came to Boston to receive information and instructions. He made them aware of the heritage they had to guard.

It is difficult to determine to what extent Dickey and the rest of the board were willing to go to protect Mrs. Eddy. In this period many were sensitive to the power of the press's delving into celebrity personal life and distorting the truth for the sake of a story. Her last years had confirmed that.

Dickey had witnessed Mrs. Eddy as a fallible older lady. He had served as a loving son as she struggled with advanced years, emerging with a deepened faith in the religious path he had chosen, stronger after having seen the unvarnished woman at close hand. Familiarity did not breed contempt, as his later writing and career proved. He had, instead, viewed her as she wished to be, as a pilgrim, never deviating from her faith into old age. He learned to follow her own admonition to find her in her writings, in her discovery. That is where he anchored his view.

But what was the board's responsibility in protecting the public perception of Mrs. Eddy? Present her as unworldly and leave the honest view he had experienced to himself? The board took the stand that the public persona as religious leader should be paramount; her personal life should remain private.

Dickey was in no hurry to write the book she had commissioned of him. To tell her story to the world—and especially that mental malpractice had murdered her—would present many difficulties. It might have been too incendiary for those precarious times. Surely the promise he had made was never far from his mind.

Other areas needed defending in the period 1911-1920—often strongly. The very essence of the church's mission was at stake. States had passed laws against spiritual healing—particularly against "Eddyism." Foreign nations and the United States Congress began to act. It was an age of focus on public health, in which water and sanitary sewer control and supervision, as noted earlier, began to be governmental functions. Medical education and practice were becoming standardized and more efficient, if not always effective, in preserving health. Supervising and testing boards were being set up to certify physicians.

The medical profession was becoming a powerful lobby. An Oklahoma senator introduced a bill to establish a national department to supervise the health of United States citizens. The bill's reach would be wide: even some medical groups were afraid of it because they did not want federal supervision. But those groups did not include the American Medical Association, which had long opposed Christian Science treatment. The issue: Should the government control the citizen's choice of method for physical healing?[3]

In 1911 the board of directors had to face New York City's growing hostility. Practitioners were brought into court after undercover officers had sought treatment, paid money, and taken notes to use in prosecutions. Judges and district attorneys, relying on archaic laws, sought convictions, and a practitioner caught in the "sting" was found guilty. The state contended it was against the law to heal through prayer and the practitioner was illegally practicing medicine. When money changed hands, he and others like him across the state were guilty of healing bodies for money through prayer. Soon the Appellate Division of the New York Supreme Court promulgated the doctrine that Christian Science practitioners must be licensed and take an exam on medical procedures after duly studying medicine. The Mother Church board became deeply involved, trying to maintain the legitimacy of Christian Science healing in the face of that untenable idea.

The New York "sting" case dragged on, with the board continuing to manage the legal defense, and finally October 3, 1916, the Court of Appeals rejected lower court decisions. It denied the power of legislatures to make it a crime to treat disease by prayer. Further decisions stretching into future decades secured the right of Christian Scientists to practice spiritual healing. The original strong focus of the board of directors of the decade after Mrs. Eddy's passing had set the pace for religious freedom principles that benefited not only Christian Scientists, but all Americans. They had little choice if the movement were to survive.

From the beginning Christian Science had been democratic in spirit; so Scientists came to have their say "to Boston." The offices were as open, at least in the early days, as Andrew Jackson's White House. And the controversies in the first decade were as numerous as the plagues of Job. In 1914 some in the field believed that Dickey's teacher, Edward Kimball, had been assailed in editorials by Associate Editor of *The Christian Science Journal*, Annie M. Knott, for derivative thinking. Although the editor, Archibald

McLellan, denied that Kimball was the target of the critical editorials, the field began talking about the "Chicago school" of Christian Science, "tainted" by Kimball's teaching, and the "Boston school" that was thought to rely more closely on Mrs Eddy's teachings. It is not clear how Dickey rowed through these troubled waters.

Warped offshoots of Christian Science continued to appear. Annie C. Bill of London believed she had "discovered" that the board structure could not be viewed as legitimate. The *Manual*, she said, had important provisions that called for Mary Baker Eddy's signature before business could proceed—the old refrain that had begun before her passing. Mrs. Bill alleged the church ought to be reorganized with a woman at the head again—namely Mrs. Bill herself, and she set up machinery in England to strike out on her own.[4]

A salary controversy also surfaced. In July, 1915, board member McLellan approached Mrs. Eddy's lawyer, Frank Streeter, to ask about the advisability of raising the board's salaries. The Mother Church by-laws specified $2,500; McLellan asked about raising the salary to $8,000 or $10,000, sharing board members' hope that they could proceed without changing the by-laws or announcing the change to the field. Complicating the matter was the fact that the board itself appeared to be split, with acrimony developing, and Streeter advised they only take controversial steps by a unanimous decision to avoid the appearance of evil and present an honest face to the movement.[5]

Questions continued to come in from the field about how to turn Mrs. Eddy's former homes into historic sites. The board seems to have cast a wary eye on what it considered to be the creation of shrines. Dickey stood firmly on the side of destroying the properties and discouraging pilgrimages, probably relying on Mrs. Eddy's express opinion that she not be turned into a "dagon."

In a related issue William D. McCrackan, one of the associate editors of the Christian Science publications, summarized his dealings with Mr. Dickey, after these events were over, evidently to set things straight. He and Dickey were eventually adversaries in litigation. But McCrackan about 1917 was interested in a number of subjects, and one of them was pyramids—an off-beat idea that became a hot topic at the church.[6]

During 1916 and 1917 one James F. Lord, who owned Mrs. Eddy's birthplace, the old Mark Baker farm, began to build a granite monument. It incorporated mystic relationships to the pyramid at Giza. Plans called for it to be placed on Lord's property to honor her. The board disapproved, issuing warnings to the field through a letter, saying "we should not center our thoughts on pyramids or personal history." Lord built it anyway.

McCrackan, a fellow classmate of Dickey's in Edward Kimball's class, came to the board's offices to bring what he believed were earnest concerns of the church membership. One of them involved the pyramid. He was preparing an article for the *Sentinel* entitled "Miracles" that Dickey reviewed. He told McCracken that he was considering refusing permission for publication because the author had mentioned pyramids, and Dickey seemed gun-shy on the subject. Eventually, however, on March 3, 1919, the article did appear, but Dickey never revoked his disapproval.

Dickey listened to many of these types of complaints. So-and-so, the committee on publication of such-and-such a town was indulging "Jesuit tendencies, dictating standards of individuals' lives." A certain member was spreading gossip about others. Dickey was likely to tell supplicants what he thought, based on his understanding of Mrs. Eddy's mission for the board. He did not like to have time wasted by whiners, and he was never accused of being mealy-mouthed.

In his account of the several visits he made to "Mr. Dickey's office," McCrackan describes him at his desk, as a "stocky, businesslike, rather defiant looking man, waiting to see what I had to say." He seemed always to want to proceed by the use of rules. At another time, he wanted to present a proposal: that he be allowed to write the biography of Mary Baker Eddy, the one that would finally set things straight. Mr. Dickey was not in favor of the plan. But then McCrackan began to tell him what was really on his mind. Things were too plodding, too business-like. "This Church should move forward by inspiration, not by rules," he asserted.

"What do you mean by inspiration?" Mr. Dickey asked angrily. He told McCrackan that he thought good business sense and sound management in the transacting of the business of The Mother Church reflected God's government. The editor told him in effect that management of the church was too rigid. Mrs. Eddy had been a woman, but now only men ran the church. Implicitly, he was calling for more women in higher position, insisting there was a "dearth of women's tears" in Boston.

He left at that, and other times, unsatisfied. In the same document, he complains that when a lady friend of his went to appeal to Dickey and the board to "handle animal magnetism better," he was reputed to have chortled and said, "Why, my dear, we directors grow fat on animal magnetism." The friend and McCrackan were shocked; Mr. Dickey was making a joke of something that was not a joke. "It will hardly become a laughing matter until all evil has come to judgment and been destroyed," he indignantly protested.

Dickey seems to have tried not to make animal magnetism a major focus as he operated on the board, but that did not keep the topic from rearing its head. Obviously he took it seriously; he had to after living at Chestnut Hill. Even McCrackan mentioned that most of his colleagues thought Mrs. Eddy had focused too much on malicious animal magnetism. Still, this man, prominent in the movement, did not like Dickey's dismissing it out of hand, if, indeed, that is what he was doing. It seems more likely that he had lived with it for quite a while in its most intense forms, and now he wished aggressive mental suggestion put into perspective in a world of complicated challenges for the movement and a cosmos where Divine Love is, in reality, all.

The authority of "the men at the top" loomed above the world of their religion like a cloud. The board notices appeared in every issue of the *Journal* and often in the *Sentinel*, outlining all sorts of divine and human concerns. They now insisted that the term, "A branch of The Mother Church, The First Church of Christ, Scientist in Boston, Massachusetts," be read at each branch church service, a demand that surprised many in the field.

Dickey stuck to the same, bulldog-like mantra: Mrs. Eddy intended for a board to exist and to continue the direction of the church. Still, this was not a church of men; God's unfolding will and the *Manual* were supposed to govern. To the extent the board listened to those agencies, the institutional church would prosper.

He expressed his understanding of what the limitations of the board were in an April, 1922, *Journal* article, "The Mother Church and the Manual."

> . . . one of the By-laws in the Manual (Art. I Sect 6) states, "The business of The Mother Church shall be transacted by its Christian Science Board of Directors." This does not mean that the Directors are at liberty to inflict their will or their desire upon the Christian Science movement. Indeed, the very opposite is true. The movement could not endure if the Directors should arbitrarily undertake to tell the members of The Mother Church how to conduct themselves. This must needs be a question of individual demonstration with which the members of the Board of Directors have no personal responsibility.

Dickey had made himself clear on the subject of board limitation almost from the time of Mrs. Eddy's passing. But many in the field believed there was constant encroachment from Boston on their individual liberties.

Trying to walk the line in leadership of the movement presented a difficult challenge. There was a day-to-day need to "transact the business of The Mother Church" while avoiding solving quandaries individual members and branch churches should themselves solve. Dickey's writings, the best source of his opinions about leadership style, indicate he considered that the problems of both individuals who were Christian Scientists and the directors themselves were solvable only by direct reliance on God.

Chapter Nine

Writing for the Movement

In January, 1916, Adam Dickey's important article "God's Law of Adjustment" appeared. It not only set forth logical argument about how God's universal law of Love operates to solve problems, it also reflected the human inadequacy the author must have felt in the face of problems to be solved and his own conviction that one must unreservedly turn management over to the divine Mind. Dickey's writings seem to always reflect some direct unfoldment in his own thought:

> When we in our helplessness reach the point where we see we are unable of ourselves to do anything, and then call upon God to aid us; when we get ready to show our willingness to abandon our own plans, our own opinions, our own sense of what ought to be done under the circumstances, and have no fear as to the consequences—then God's law will take possession of and govern the whole situation. . . . When we understand that infinite Mind is the ruler of the universe, that every idea of God is forever in its proper place, that no condition or circumstance can arise whereby a mistake can find lodgment in God's plan, then we have the complete assurance that God is capable of adjusting everything as it should be. . . .

There was great need for that sort of wisdom. Management of the church was growing much more complicated than in the days when a few students met in a parlor in Lynn—or even when communion services were held for joyous students at the Boston church and its Extension. Part of the challenge was just the multiplication of members and the questions coming at the board. Only four years after Mrs. Eddy's passing the "transacting of business" of the board had grown so complex that they had to meet several times a week. As the original designations of responsibility set up by the *Church Manual* had to be expanded; more people came to work at the church headquarters. The cabinet government had by 1915 evolved into a bureaucracy with workers and sub-workers.

There was work for them to do. A major challenge came from far beyond Boston. World War I had erupted across Europe, and in 1914 The Christian Science Board of Directors sent a member of the Board of Lectureship abroad to organize relief efforts. The *Sentinel* announced that a War Relief Fund was being set up and donations would be accepted. Dickey was still Treasurer at the time. William D. McCrackan, the publications editor who had visited Mr. Dickey at headquarters, headed up the effort abroad and sailed from New York on December 5. The fund's help soon extended to non-Scientists, as the devastation in Europe became wide-spread. The Mother Church intended to aid not only the lands of the Allies, but also those of Germany and Hungary, their enemies. Centers set up in various nations were kept busy supplying funds for refugees and the wounded.

When the United States entered the war in 1917, more appeals were made so the fund could continue in an expanded fashion, serving soldiers in their camps. Chaplains-at-large were commissioned. Soon Christian Science workers were visiting camps in war areas, conducting services and sharing literature.[1] Newspapers praised the efforts of Christian Scientists, who showed their charitable spirit in this and other relief projects. It was part of a natural evolution of the Church into a more-or-less respected denomination that cooperated with others and involved itself in the concerns of a complicated world.

Dickey's article "Preparedness" appeared in the May 18, 1918, *Christian Science Sentinel*. It was applicable to the war relief efforts the church was making, and encouraged a right attitude towards the challenges of war. Calling for not only practical preparedness in the face of the needs of the present situation, he tells the reader that "It is in knowing how to think rightly that true preparedness consists." He further states:

> Jesus did not begin his great life work until he had spent many years in preparation. He had doubtless been educated at his mother's knee and there taught the reverence for the law of God which he displayed in after years. He knew that God was his Father, and that as the offspring of divine intelligence he shared the wisdom and power of his Father. After the Holy Ghost had descended upon him he withdrew to the wilderness there to prove to himself that he had the right idea of God and that he was prepared to give it to the world. . . his close walk with God and his devotion to the will of his Father was what made him ready for the service that was his to perform.

He goes on:

In the case of our own dearly beloved leader, she tells us how God had been graciously preparing her during many years for the reception of the revelation of Christian Science (see Science and Health p. 107) As the world reckons time she was forty-five years of age when this discovery came to her, and during the following forty-four years she wrote Science and Health with Key to the Scriptures and her other writing, founded the Christian Science movement, and led it to its present successful and progressive stage of development. And now do we think that we shall win our battles without due preparation, and without faithful application and devotion to the demands of God?

The article exhorts all to press on with deeper conviction and more consecrated prayer and study because the "foe in ambush" was challenging the divine idea. "The battle is on today, both mentally and physically, and we are in the midst of it."

While he was "in the midst of it" not only with the wartime effort but also in the ongoing contentious debates and controversies at church headquarters, Dickey wrote some of his strongest articles for the Christian Science publications. This small collection would eventually stand among the clearest statements of Christian Science, the best and most popular articles originated by one of Mrs. Eddy's followers.

"God's Law of Adjustment," in *The Christian Science Journal*, January, 1916, is written in the typically closely reasoned, and unornamental style mentioned before, a style that reflected the author's approach to life. Make the point early, develop it with down-to-earth examples and logic, then reiterate the point, slightly advancing the argument until the reader is convinced. "God's Law of Adjustment" is an effective example of the "gradually developing your point through extended iteration" variant of the occasional essay. McCrackan might have said it proceeded not by inspiration but by the rules, but it has both.

Early on Dickey asks the reader to agree with certain premises: that God works through laws and that His laws are the only governing principles. He next asserts that if all of God's laws govern existence, our job is to connect ourselves with them to live harmoniously.

We have declared the truth, God's truth—and that truth of God is the law of annihilation, obliteration and elimination to everything that is unlike Him. When we have stated this truth, and applied it as taught in Christian Science, to any discordant belief with which we are confronted, we have done all that we can do and all this necessary for us to do in the destruction of any manifestation of that error that ever claimed to exist.

And, as he often stated, when you have said that, you have said everything there is to say.

He cites specific instances in which a person can be placed in extreme conditions and yet not be separated from remedy, as the divine law of God adjusts the circumstances to harmony. Dickey's first, and best known, example of dire circumstances that God can correct is that of a man "drowning in mid-ocean." A divine law, when appealed to, can bring about his rescue. The second example in the 1916 version reads as follows: "If a man were in prison, there is a law of God which is applicable to his condition and which, if properly applied, would procure his release." Perhaps he was thinking of Paul and Silas in Acts 16, bursting from prison with God's help. The prison passage is eliminated in subsequent versions, and it is not difficult to see how some readers may have misunderstood it. What if a person were imprisoned according to the justice system? What if he or she did the crime and needed to pay the price? "Let human justice pattern the divine," Mrs. Eddy writes.

Dickey varies his main point, stating that we do not need to know exactly how the law of God will operate in each case to do the adjustment, that we should not be in the position of telling the divine Mind how to let "God's will be done," that activating God's law of adjustment, which is ever operative, requires complete surrender of self to it.

A few paragraphs near the end seem particularly poignant in light of Dickey's unsought role as the spokesman of the board:

> What then are we to do when we find ourselves involved in a controversy, in a dispute, or in an unpleasant situation of any kind? What are we to do when we have been attacked and maligned, misrepresented or abused? Should we endeavor to return in kind what has been done to us? This would not be appealing to God's law of adjustment. So long as we endeavor to settle the difficulty ourselves, we are interfering with the action of the law of God. Under any circumstance of this kind, it will avail us nothing to fight back. We simply show our human weakness when we take the matter into our own hands and attempt either to punish our enemies or to extricate ourselves through any virtue of our own.

Another section of the 1916 version has been removed from modern reprints; it specifically dealt with Jesus' injunctions to "bless those that curse you" and turn the other cheek. Dickey no doubt believed that no amount of reaffirming Jesus' direct commands to forgive was too much, given the circumstances he and the Christian Science movement were living through, but later editors eliminated them.

Even with the writing that was published during these years and which brought him recognition, he stumbled along, making enemies, trying to avoid jealousy, and defending Mrs. Eddy's reputation at a time all the board members believed hints of her struggles should be curtailed. His leadership was that of a good, but average, man trying hard, sometimes missing the mark. Adelaide Still told of being implored by Dickey to keep the details of Mrs. Eddy's frailty to herself, even in court.[2]

Most of all, he was trying to decide how much control of the church was too much, and he and the other board members did not get it right all of the time. As the decade wound down, people wrote more frequently asking the board about the most trivial of details in their church services, wanting to know what to say, when to say it, what to wear, when to wear it and so forth. And since the supplicants often seemed like sheep without a shepherd, in spite of the board's best intentions, no doubt, about letting Christian Scientists chart out their own paths with God, they often caved in and gave advice.

In 1917 a request was made to the field to forward any personal letters of Mary Baker Eddy to Boston.[3] Although the board insisted the collecting of letters was to archive them, some believed it was to control information. The action was typical of some that suggested attempts to control the field.

More importantly, the board was also deciding by about 1916 what the nature of "authorized" information would be—who was putting out "un-authorized" ideas and literature—and reprimanding or disciplining those who deviated from "standards." It was the beginning of over-direction that in the 1930s and 1940s reached proportions that distressed many, caused some prominent lecturers and teachers to withdraw from membership, and eventuated in what can only be called suppression of dissent and over-control of branch churches. Still, the board did what they deemed best. Much that they did turned out to be right.

Chapter Ten

The Great Litigation: Lawyers "Vs. Dickey"

In 1917 the defense of Christian Science took on importance that dwarfed the day-to-day problems of church expansion in the world. The challenge was only partly from "without," from periodicals and books and more importantly from state legislatures and national assemblies. The greatest challenge came from within—with a series of lawsuits since called "The Great Litigation."

Beyond the claim that church government should not be functioning because Mrs. Eddy's name was on by-laws that required her approval of business and she was not there, beyond the squabbles over how far The Mother Church interfered in branch church and individual lives—there was a more serious and ominous split. Unless the board solved it, there might not be a Christian Science movement.

The Christian Science Publishing Society trustees challenged the board of The First Church of Christ, Scientist, in Boston. Its struggle to prevail in the courts occupied both important agencies for much of the time period 1919-1921. At the time of this litigation Dickey was considered to be the church's spokesman and leading defender and was chairman of the board when the first legal actions were taken.

The controversy had some of its roots in personal animosity, that quality Mrs. Eddy had so carefully warned about in the *Manual* in "A Rule for Motives and Acts." But it also involved two groups of devoted Christian Scientists who believed they were following their leader's intents for her church.

The Publishing Society and its trustees were an essential part of the structure of institutional Christian Science because they controlled the publication of books and the influential and lucrative periodicals. The group began to take a divergent path from the board midway in the decade after the leader's passing.

The board, asserting its responsibility in the movement for all business, pressed the Publishing Society trustees on a number of matters, including specifics of publication and staffing, and the Publishing Society became increasingly resistant.

One of its newer trustees, Lamont Rowlands, had been named a trustee in August, 1917. He did not attend meetings regularly and seemed from the beginning to flaunt the will of the board.

Rowlands had proposed, and the other trustees had adopted, a policy that would permit the Society to publish cards of practitioners and branch churches not recognized by the directors of The Mother Church. This policy was in violation of the *Church Manual*, and the board remonstrated. Other issues arose in which the trustees demonstrated that they believed themselves independent of the church; the board continued to try to persuade them to accede for the good of the movement, an effort which did not succeed.

The trustees' assertion of independence rested on their belief, soon to be transformed into legal action, that Mrs. Eddy's Deed of Trust that set the trusteeship up had precedence over the *Manual* by-laws. They contended that the Deed of Trust gave them independent authority.

March 17, 1919, the board of The Mother Church passed a resolution dismissing Lamont Rowlands under Article XXV, sections 3 and 5 of the *Manual*. A letter next day instructed the trustees to appoint a new member. They refused, and the matter sat for a short while.

But surprisingly, the board of directors also acted against one of its own at the same time, John V. Dittemore, who had been on the board since 1909, and had become adamant in his belief that the board members were acting too slowly and weakly against the trustees. He had some justification in his contention: at times they seemed frozen in place.

Adding to his disaffection were the residual effects of the salary controversy. The board had raised its salary. Dittemore opposed the increase at every turn. He contended that the board was exceeding its *Manual*-authorized authority when it claimed it needed more money for the increased management load. The board, he said in effect, should function as a cabinet and not as a set of managing bureaucrats.[1]

Dickey and the others witnessed Dittemore's treating them with increasing contempt and finally responded. In their resolution of dismissal they contended that he had acted on his own, instructed committees on publication in ways contrary to the group will, talked outside board meetings about what went on, written acrimonious letters, refused to vote, and . . .

> Whereas Mr. Dittemore has ceased to maintain towards the other members of this Board an attitude of unity, cooperation, equality and Christian fellowship, and has habitually adopted

the opposite attitude, so that it has become extremely difficult
for this Board to perform its functions. . .

they were forced to dismiss him.[2] Charges were exchanged, other pioneers
in the movement became involved. William McCrackan was dismissed as
publications editor and bitter debates ensued. Judge Smith sent a letter that
appeared in the *Boston Herald* explaining the board's position. The board
might be faulted during this period for not handling publicity well, both to
non-Science newspapers and to Christian Scientists across the world.

By March, 1919, the trustees had brought suit against the board of The
Mother Church, demanding that they be subpoenaed, arrested, and haled
into court for slandering them in the press and in the eyes of the movement.
In June the directors were found guilty of contempt.

Actions in Equity went before the court, with a Master appointed to
hear testimony and render a judgment. February 20, 1920, the Master ruled
that Rowlands's removal was not lawfully effected by the resolution adopted
on March 17, 1919. The board did not have the authority to dismiss him, in
spite of the *Manual* provision that allowed them to do so, and he remained
a trustee. The board was enjoined not to try to subordinate the actions of
the trustees to the board, nor to compel the resignation of the trustees. Mrs.
Eddy's deed of January 25, 1898, prevailed at this time.

But when the board asked to have articles placed in the *Monitor*, the
Sentinel, and the *Journal* to express some of their views, the Publishing Society refused. An injunction limited the board from imposing authority over
the Publishing Society.

Dittemore had also sued. His bill of complaint, filed April 29, 1919,
alleged that the board had not fulfilled its duties in "protecting the interests
of the members of the Church as Trust beneficiaries" because it did not act
decisively against the Publishing Society trustees who were guilty of "gross
waste and extravagance in the administration of their trust."

He further alleged that because he had stood for firm action against
the trustees, he had been dismissed "without notice or hearing."

The board of directors answered and published its legal reply, filed
May 15, 1919, for the field from its offices at 105 Falmouth Street. They answered in detail certain of Dittemore's allegations about misappropriation
of funds and mismanagement at the board level, then went on to one of the
key allegations: that the board had "private dealings" with the trustees in an
attempt to quietly settle the dispute, thus avoiding adverse publicity.

July 24, 1919, Dickey testified that he had not compromised the stern
standards the board (especially Dittemore) had wished enforced just for the
sake of conciliation. "Dickey Gets Severe Cross-Examination" the headline
in the *Boston Globe* read. Lawyers for the trustees had grilled Dickey on this

day in court, also.[3]

The Master found that Dittemore's dismissal, too, had not been justified. This period in 1919-20 was a terrible challenge for Dickey, James A. Neal, Edward A. Merritt, William R. Rathvon and Annie M. Knott, who constituted the board of The Mother Church. Most often, however, Dickey came to personify the movement in the eyes of the public because his was the name known, cited in the lawsuits as first defendant in these legal matters and covered in the newspapers as a sort of "Mr. Christian Science."

Those in the field, most supporting the board, responded when the Master found against the board in 1920 with shock and cancellation of their subscriptions to the Christian Science publications.

In November, 1920, the Supreme Judicial Court of Massachusetts met to hear arguments of lawyers representing Dittemore, the directors, and the trustees. It was to be a testing, an appeal, of the Master's ruling.

On November 29, the nationally famous lawyer, Charles Evans Hughes, began to present the trustees' case: When Mary Baker Eddy granted the Deed of Trust, he said, she turned over all authority for publication of Christian Science literature to the trustees. That had been her intent, an intent that the deed itself honored. She did not, he alleged, give power over the trustees to the board of directors. The directors in point of fact had no power over that self-perpetuating board she had set up with the specific intent, Hughes contended, that it not be subject to the board of The Mother Church.

John L. Bates, representing the directors, did not, of course, agree. The authority for the entire church had passed from the First Members (who were the first church, but were superseded by the board of directors in 1898) to the board of directors, and with them the authority of the church rested.

The directors alone had the right to remove a trustee of the Publishing Society. "It will be claimed that this was two boards, one to be a check on the other. That element does not seem to exist here," Bates reasoned.

After a seemingly endless year, the Supreme Court, to the great joy of the directors and the majority of those in the movement, sustained the *Manual* and the directors.

> The edition of the *Manual* which was in use on January 25, 1898, the date of the Trust Deed, was designated the seventh . . .

> It is manifest that the trust deed was intended to be subject, so far as it concerned the officers of the Church and their powers and duties touching upon the disbursement of the net income paid by the Trustees to the Treasurer of the Church to

such changes as the occasion might require to be made in the
Manual . . .

the Court said, and added:

> Although the Trustees under the Trust Deed were given ex-
> tensive powers concerning the publication of the so-called litera-
> ture of the Church, nevertheless they were not the final arbiters
> concerning these matters, because they might be removed from
> office by other Church authorities "for such reason" as to other
> Church authorities "may seem expedient."

The *Boston Post* headlined its November 24, 1921, edition "Christian
Science Directors Upheld as Church Heads," and the subhead was "Manual
is Supreme." Adam Dickey said that Thanksgiving was the best he and the
whole movement had ever known.[4]

The trustees agreed to submit to the board. And business in Boston began again, at a gradually accelerating pace. Almost immediately subscriptions
to the publications resumed and grew rapidly. Societies and new churches
again began to apply for recognition.

It is odd that neither Hughes nor the board seemed to realize the central truth of the controversy, a set of historical facts that could have saved
everybody a great deal of trouble. Dickey himself may not have known the
full history of the Deeds of Trust. At any rate, it is not clear why this history
was not introduced on either side.

One of today's scholars of the movement, Keith McNeil, has explained
the historical background that impacted this Publishing Society controversy:

> The history of the Christian Science Publishing Society ac-
> tually starts back in 1875, when Mrs. Eddy (then Mrs. Glover)
> had her first edition of *Science and Health* published by the "Chris-
> tian Science Publishing Company." This was an unincorporated,
> loose organization of a few individuals and was short-lived. Dur-
> ing the next fourteen years the publication of Christian Science
> material (which was approved by her) was done by Mrs. Eddy,
> her husband, Asa G. Eddy, or those under her direct supervision.
> However, at the fourth annual meeting of the National Christian
> Science Association (NCSA) in 1889, Mrs. Eddy turned over the
> ownership of *The Christian Science Journal* to the NCSA. This was
> part of an overall attempt by Mrs. Eddy to place more respon-
> sibility on Christian Scientists. The NCSA set up a "Publishing
> committee" to handle the publication of the *Journal*.
>
> In 1893 the *Journal* ownership was returned to Mrs. Eddy,

but by this time the sale of Christian Science literature had become an increasingly important business. The responsibility for publishing most of her writings along with other Christian Science periodicals, and the increasing financial revenue that was flowing in meant that this was a business enterprise that could no longer be taken for granted. On December 7, 1896, Mrs. Eddy recommended that the "Christian Science Publishing Society" be incorporated; however various delays pushed back the actual date of incorporation to April 3, 1897. It should be noted that Mrs. Eddy did not own the stock of the corporation.

By this time it became apparent to Mrs. Eddy that certain risk existed if she did not have ultimate control of the publishing of Christian Science literature, especially her own writings. While she was more willing to leave the routine business aspect of publishing to others, she did not want to have the ultimate decisions on content and related issues left up to others.

The easiest solution would have been to have The Mother Church own the Christian Science Publishing Society business. In that way she could have controlled the publishing activities in the same way that she effectively had control over the church activities. This was the solution Mrs. Eddy wanted. However, there were two significant roadblocks to the approach. The first was the concern that should the Publishing Society be swallowed up by the church, the name "Christian Science Publishing Society" could be taken by others, such as those who defected from the church in 1888 and started their own short-lived Christian Science periodical. But the more important obstacle was a legal one.

When the church reorganized in 1892, it was done under Chapter 39, Section I of the Public Statues of Massachusetts, The pertinent section of that chapter read in part

"The income of the grants or donations made to or for the use of any one church shall not exceed $2,000 a year exclusive of the income to any parsonage lands granted to or for the use of the ministry."

The statute did not prevent gifts of over $2,000, rather it prevented gifts or business or other interests that produced income in excess of $2,000 annually, excluding gifts of land to the church or "ministry."

Since the Christian Science Publishing Society was producing income in excess of that, it was not possible to give it to the church, although the land that it was on could be given to The Mother Church.

The answer came to Mrs. Eddy to have the Publishing Society corporation dissolved and the assets sold to her. Then she
could create a trust with handpicked trustees who could be trusted to work under her direction. Since the law did not require the
land to be kept from the church, she could create a separate trust
deed for the land under the Publishing Society, which was at that
time next door to the edifice of The Mother Church. While this
was simple in concept, it was actually a very complicated transac-
tion, but it was all accomplished in January, 1898.

So this was not, then, as was later claimed, the leader's spiritual plan to
keep authority in the church balanced by setting up two competing agencies
with equal power. The Trust was plain and simply a legal idea to protect the
money-earning capacities of the periodicals under the general umbrella of
The Mother Church, while safeguarding Mrs. Eddy's own editorial say-so.

Dickey was again present at his post during the Great Litigation. Others on the board deserve credit for perseverance and prayer, but it was Dickey
whose name was most closely associated with the cases and final settlement.
He may bear responsibility for the board's ineptness at times, too, failing to
seize the advantage, bungling publicity, and over-agitating the field. But, on
the whole, he comes across positively. Again, his close association with Mrs.
Eddy in her final years, his business-like handling of emotionally-charged
affairs, and his "bulldog-like" loyalty were valued by the rest of the board
members as well as by the field at large.

Norman Beasley, whose book *The Continuing Spirit* deals with the movement in the years after Mrs. Eddy, states: "It was not a calm period in the
history of the Christian Science Movement."[5] If one served on the board at
that time, this statement would have seemed an understatement. Dickey was
the right man to exert steady influence during this difficult time. That Dittemore did not excoriate him in his 1932 book done with Ernest Sutherland
Bates the way he did others may testify to a degree of respect he preserved
for the man who headed the board when he was dismissed.

Dickey had helped see the board through the Red Sea. He remained
at his post for five more years after the settlement, no doubt viewing with
gratitude the continued growth of the movement in something of a promised land.

Adam H. Dickey's new house on grounds that once belonged to Mrs. John M. (Mary Beecher) Longyear.
Courtesy Keith McNeil Collection

Mr. Dickey at the time he served on the Board of Directors.
Courtesy Elizabeth Dickey
Herman Collection

Mr. Dickey's own 1906 view of the original First Church of Christ, Scientist in Boston and the Extension.

Courtesy Elizabeth Dickey Herman Collection

Chapter Eleven

Peaceful Living Near Longyear

Adam Dickey had continued to keep in touch with his close, individualistic family. Mrs. Eddy had reluctantly given him some leave time during his stay with her, and he had made two visits to Kansas City in 1910, one for his parents' Golden Wedding celebration, one for the court case in October. He missed the sendoff of his father's last adventure. In December of that year, when Dickey was most needed in Boston, his father and Nathaniel's brother Joseph, began a trip down the Mississippi to New Orleans: eventual destination, Florida.

The *Kansas City Republic* printed photos of the two distinguished gentlemen with goatees, preparing to board the "yacht *Unique*" from St. Louis to New Orleans, photos Adam Dickey preserved in his personal effects. "At [New Orleans]" the newspaper went on, "they will board a train for Mobile, and from there will take a Mallory line vessel to their destination."

Nathaniel Dickey discussed the trip with a newspaper reporter:

> Yes, we two youngsters are going to try our hands at yachting down the stream. While we are not what might be classed as old roosters, still we are not "young broilers," although we are quite tender as yet. We are probably old enough to take care of ourselves.

The boat taking them to New Orleans had been detained in St. Louis hung up on a sandbar, and had to be fitted for a new rudder. Nathaniel assured his friends the octogenarians would be "taking it easy" until the yacht was ready.

The same newspaper article reported that Walter Dickey owned the yacht and was "the former chairman of the Republican State committee." His mansion on the hill had been completed after years in construction. Walter's son Kenneth in his usual critical way described the house as a "huge, cold, set piece, mausoleum sort of place. One got the impression that if you sat in a chair or walked over an inch thick rug, it would be best to do so with care."

Walter was involving himself in a cabinet and fixture company, curbing and walks, a telephone business in competition with Bell, real estate, trap shooting, and the Navigation Company, which owned the yacht his father and uncle took on the Mississippi. But these ventures were, according to his son in *A Man with Clay Feet*, draining rather than adding to his fortune. Although W.S. Dickey Clay Manufacturing Company continued to be a money-maker, Walter's tendency to invest in speculative ventures that would prove unsuccessful was beginning to show. His real interest was Republican politics, and he spent much time building the machines both in Kansas City and throughout the state.

The Dickeys' sister Lillian had fulfilled her dream by 1915 and headed west. This independent-minded woman had taken up a claim in Havre, Montana, and intended to turn it into a successful flax seed and wheat farm. Living in a shack for a while, she began outfitting the place, purchasing a surrey, horses, and farm machinery, hiring "hands," and building a small house. Since temperatures dipped to 15 below zero in Montana, she returned to Kansas City in the winter at first, later staying on the ranch all year. She sent many Kodak box camera photos home, which the Dickeys kept in their collection.

Nathaniel Dickey died in 1911, and his son Adam said of him in his *Memoirs*, "I never knew a better man than my father." The family still tells the story of outrage when Walter Dickey came to his father's deathbed and had him sign over his remaining interest in family ventures to him.

Lillian and Adam Dickey needed a permanent home in the Boston area and purchased property from Mary Beecher Longyear at Fisher Hill in Brookline.[1] It stood on a terrace below the Longyear home and was described as a "modern house." Next to the Dickeys' house was that of Archibald McLellan. Family visitors from Kansas City could see the wide, open rooms with terraces and gardens of a comfortable, but not ostentatious, house. Of special interest, Elizabeth Dickey Herman told her friends after she visited, was an oriental room with imports from Asia.

Dickey continued class teaching during the years he served on the board and as its Treasurer. From 1912 to 1923 his classes and association met in Boston. Students later reported that wife Lillian sat on the podium with him as he gave his addresses, handing him materials he needed.[2]

A particular treatment, so typical of his "One mind, that is all" metaphysics, shared with students, was eventually given to the Mary Baker Eddy Library.

Treatment

There is one infinite Mind. One ever present, eternal all in-clusive, self-sustaining Mind, which depends upon nothing else for existence. This infinite Mind is the only Power, the only Cre-ator, the Cause, the Law, the Government, the divine Principle of all that really exists.

Mind creates and knows ideas only, and is capable of pro-ducing nothing unlike Itself. If Mind is Infinite and All, then no finite or limited sense of Mind can possibly exist. There is no mortal mind, no evil mind, and that which claims to be tempo-ral and mortal is illusion only. The belief that there is another mind beside God, is not a creator and can have no intelligence power or cause. "If Mind is within and without all things, then all is Mind, and this definition is scientific." If Mind had no expression it would have no existence, no entity, and would be forever unknown; but Mind is known, express and manifested, therefore "All is infinite Mind, and its infinite manifestation." (S&H.) and all that exists must be either Mind, or that which expresses Mind. Matter is not Mind, does not represent Mind, therefore its existence is a myth and all the beliefs that claim to go with matter are unreal.[3]

The Dickeys' life was now comfortable, with the salary increase on the board, and the metaphysical questions around this level of comfort may have been reflected in the article "Possession," which appeared in *The Christian Science Journal* as the lead article, June, 1917.

There is a belief among mortals that they can become the privileged possessors or owners of something. When through the usual process of law a man acquires property, he has a strong de-sire to erect a fence around it, and to keep everybody else away. Then follows the belief, which is universally acknowledged, that he owns a certain amount of the earth's surface and that the law protects and defends him in proving possession thereof. He builds a house and occupies it, calls it his own, and no one is per-mitted to approach or to enter it contrary to his wishes without being considered a trespasser. In our present degree of develop-ment it is generally understood that property is something which should have an owner; that the earth and all that is contained

therein may be divided into parts and parcels, and that different individuals may claim possession of more or less of it to the
exclusion of others.

The article advances the argument that no one can own possessions
because they are ideas of God in reality. Just as numbers are ideas and be-
long to everybody, he asserts, so eventually will we all realize that what we
see as parcels of land and individual domains are spiritual ideas, and the
possession of all. It is a premise rather like the American Indian's concept of
land as the gift of the Great Spirit. Harmonious functioning of any part of
what we regard as our own businesses and property depends on our ability
to exchange our concepts of them as limited to personal ownership and to
turn their management over to God, divine Mind.

Dickey develops his argument that all that exists are the ideas of God,
divine Mind in various forms and therefore possessed by Mind and collec-
tively by his spiritual idea, man. He discusses parts of the body as originating
and perfect in Mind:

> In mortal mind's method of thinking, thoughts are exter-
> nalized as matter and are called the body. When we understand
> this, and grasp what Mrs. Eddy teaches in regard to the exter-
> nalization of thought, we shall see that our bodies are nothing
> more or less that the outward expression of our thought. . . what
> Mind knows about the thing we call eye is all there is to it [as
> the light of the body, as Jesus said, a spiritual concept]. This is
> also true in regard to what mortal mind calls heart, liver, lungs
> and all else that goes to make up the so-called material body. . . .
> Inasmuch as there is only one right idea of everything, there is
> only one right concept of stomach. It is not made of matter; it
> is not a material thing. It is a mental concept and as such has its
> right place in the divine Mind. Any other concept of stomach is
> false and misleading.

He extends the thought of possession to include what one possesses in
thought, about the body, which he says can only be what Mind knows.

The McCrackan document states about "Possession" that, "It was
characteristic of the spirit of destructive criticism already then injected into
the ranks from the outside that Dickey's article was not everywhere hailed
with joy. . . there was a certain amount of splitting of hairs about it."

The article was gone over before it came out in booklet form. Editing
shifted some of the language about the bodily parts around, eliminated a
bit of it, and more than once chose strong alternative quotations of Mrs.
Eddy to back up several arguments. It also streamlined language. Most of the
work, however, remains about the same as Adam Dickey wrote it.

Octogenarian Brothers on Trip

NATHANIEL DICKEY ◊ ◊ ◊ JOSEPH DICKEY

The "young broilers," Nathaniel and his brother Joseph, prepare for their great yachting adventure.
Courtesy Elizabeth Dickey Herman Collection

Elizabeth Simpson Dickey, wife of Nathaniel and mother of Adam H. Dickey, who seemed to favor his mother in looks.
Courtesy Elizabeth Dickey Herman Collection

Fred and "Lilla" Dickey, Adam's brother and sister, after preparing for their trip to Havre, Montana, sent their brother this snapshot.
Courtesy Elizabeth Dickey Herman Collection

Chapter Twelve

Finally to the Task

It had been twelve years since his "Dearly beloved leader" had summoned him, then made a request that Mr. Dickey write a book explaining that she had been mentally murdered.Up to this time he had not done so.

Events for the board of directors from 1911 to 1920 had been momentous, consuming time and concentration. Growing the church and defending it had been two full-time jobs.

Then there was the matter of the leader's reputation, a matter of increased focus after 1920. The Wilbur book stood as a glowing testimony to the goodness of a woman without personal problems. New books with a very different view were about to come out. Dittemore was preparing to write, using the collection he had amassed, taking documents as he could find them. He would not be sparing in his view, distorted by his own animosity. Others could be more ruinous, as far as the board could see, divulging parts of her life that were controversial. Was the world ready to see "Mary" the person? Did the world really need a truthful biography?

But what was truth? It was in many cases a matter of interpretation. You could see the stories of friends falling away, calling their leader bossy or unreasonable as evidence of too strong a personality or even of instability. Or, as Dickey believed, you could see her following her destiny and expecting a good deal of all around her. If she called for action against malicious animal magnetism and was adamant about it, she had had reason to, considering the world's attack.

Further complicating the matter was Mrs. Eddy's own reluctance during the latter years of her life to have her biography written.

Historian Keith McNeil has summarized her complicated but definite views on having a biography written from her own words:

> In reply to your kind request that you be allowed to sketch
> my history will say I have learned of the logic of events that none
> but a thorough Christian Scientist can do this.—Feb. 28, 1898.

[Letter to Henry Robinson, former mayor of Concord, N.H. and someone who had interviewed Mrs. Eddy in the past and recorded her history.]

I have read your article with pleasure. Mr. . . . has not the knowledge of the past history of my struggles and what the cost of bringing C.S. to this triumphal hour [has been.] My students, even know little more of what I have met for them and still am meeting, than the babe in his mother's arms knows of her travail to bring forth this babe, a toil to bring him up to manhood~Feb 8, 1901 [Letter to August E. Stetson. The blanked-out name in the Stetson book *Sermons and Other Writings,* is believed to refer to Irving Tomlinson.]

You look up my history as you have opportunity but keep me out of mind and when there is less outside pressure I will let you know and then you can go to Mr. McCraken [i.e. William D. McCrackan] give him all your Mss and tell him all you know of me and let him correct and compile my History and write it out in full. Meanwhile, I will pay you or you and he may own the copyright together which will make you both an income worth owning. ~September 16, 1902, [Letter to Irving C. Tomlinson].

I thank you. My history dolorosa you have depicted, it brought my tears, it will bring others!—June 21, 1903. [letter to John B. Willis.This is evidently related to his contribution of a biographical sketch of her life in the New Hampshire book, *State Builders.*]

Mr. [Edward] Kimball has shown me your statement on my life prepared for the *Boston Herald.* I thank you and I love you but the ferment of this hour in our Cause requires much wisdom prayer and sacrifice of us all. I cannot permit publication now but when God in His infinite wisdom directs me I shall risk even these words of love and praise to be placed upon the altar before the eyes of sinful humanity. With my thanks and my love . . . December 4, 1904 [Letter to Edward and Caroline Bates].

I wish I could expose every period of my earth-life for the benefit of the race. I think our one God knew best whom he appointed to reveal the riches of His love and wisdom to poor humanity.~March 13, 1907 [Letter to L. Emogene Moore].

I am not willing to have my history written now and cannot spare a thought for it. The present is enough for one now to deal with.—March 25, 1908 [letter to Alfred Farlow].

Put it into the public notice that I forbid the publication of my history or autobiography [sic] by Sibyl Wilbur or any other person without my written endorsement or consent.—August 29, 1908 [letter to Alfred Farlow].

Your history of me was not even given to me to read. And I am determined that my history or autobiography shall not be written at this date—[Undated, unsigned letter probably late August, 1908, from Mrs. Eddy to Miss Sybil[sic] Wilbur. The letter was given to Alfred Farlow and it was collected in Irving Tomlinson's reminiscence material. While not in Mrs. Eddy's handwriting, it was on her Chestnut Hill stationery.]

With this background, Dickey would have to determine just what "a history of what has transpired in your experiences with me" would entail. He must have been relieved that his mission was only to cover the years 1908-1910; others would have to take up the story before that. He did not pretend to be a historian, or a professional writer. He could only do his straight-forward best.

But beyond the questions of time period and style were the questions of exactly what Mrs. Eddy wanted told. Clearly, in dealing with others she had wished the story to deal in depth with her character, to dig deeply, giving many facets. She seemed to want to include something of the metaphysical learning she conveyed to her household family, her "Divinity Course," as she called it. And in the original exchange, when he swore before God he would "write a history of what I have seen, and heard from your lips, concerning your life," he thought that some background stories she had shared could be included. Most important, he knew her hope that the world, especially Christian Scientists, would understand the pressures and crosses she bore during that time. This was a decent and understandable goal, in keeping with her oft-stated views of herself.

He could not have been unaware, though, that to honor that emphasis on suffering for the cause, to show her as a vulnerable part of "mankind," might not be received well at the board level. He would be in conflict with the very people he had worked so closely with for over ten years. But he went ahead anyway. Dickey had shown himself a person of integrity from the time he was a small boy. His father had described him as open-faced and open-hearted, willing to shake his fist at the wrong and stand for the right. That reputation had held during the trying times of litigation and expansion.

He knew that the sugar-coated view of Mrs. Eddy was not true. This woman he had come to know and love as well as admire as spiritual leader, was many-sided. She didn't want to be seen as a bisque-faced doll, parroting platitudes. The trials she endured were part of her experience and the experience of any "sincere seeker of truth," and that was an important point of Christian Science she did not want her followers to miss. On the other hand, the story he had to tell was in its essence a positive one, showing her caring for her own, courageous, insightful, spontaneous in responding to God's commands. He decided to tell the story in a simple, friend-to-friend way. He would keep the promise; he would share the truth as he had lived it, only eliminating some of the more sensational parts of the leader's struggle.

Ultimately his choice had to have been the right one. Christian Science had always taught that Truth with a capital "T" is expressed as truth with a small one, seen in every facet of life, lived in the smallest details. If mankind could not live with the fuller portrait of Mary Baker Eddy, it needed to. He was not creating the full picture, but he was playing a part in that process.

His decision to write *Memoirs of Mary Baker Eddy* in an unvarnished fashion was a departure for the movement. It is true that it gave ammunition to the later biographers bent on destroying her reputation, like Edwin Franden Dakin, who wrote a vilifying, Freudian biography in 1929. But it also paved the way for the scholarly life stories of Mary Baker Eddy done by Robert Peel and Gillian Gill. These balanced versions of her life changed the way America thought about the founder of Christian Science. Because when her life is examined in the light of truth, she comes across as supremely spiritual, devoted to the cause she established—loving, loyal, vitally intelligent—the most remarkable woman of nineteenth century America. And if the "Mary" in her was also hard-headed, a little prideful, sometimes distressed, frustrated with ineptness, and tormented by the communal beliefs of evil, we can take that, too. Adam Dickey singlehandedly took that stand for the movement, and it may have been his greatest contribution.

And so he began to write from notes made in a little journal book during his stay in the household, from transcripts of conversations, and from his memory.[1]

Right away, following historical information about himself and as a sort of introduction, he gives the charge to write the book, including Mrs. Eddy's request to say that she was mentally murdered in a section called "A Commission from Mrs. Eddy." In addition to giving an explanation for his candor, in this section he protects himself by attributing the necessity for writing to her. In "The Journey East" he speaks of the trip and gives impressions of the household "family" and Chestnut Hill.

"First Meeting with Mrs. Eddy" begins the truth-telling: he was to find out that though often stalwart, she sometimes bent beneath her load of care and often called for aid against the forces of malicious animal magnetism.

"'General Quarters' at Home" tells of the night watches against "M.A.M." needed by the leader when particularly important issues were to be solved or other problems occurred.

"The Ideal of Orderliness and Regularity" shows Mrs. Eddy's penchant for neatness and order in her room arrangements, timing of household routines, and personal appearance; "Generosity—A Lifelong Characteristic" shows her giving gifts to friends and neighbors.

"'Wit, Humor and Enduring Vivacity'—Accuracy in Thought and Deed" describes her habits of exactness in her own writing, and "Reluctance of Mrs. Eddy to Change Her Writings in Response to Criticisms" and "Changes in the Writing" give examples of her pondering exact words and insisting on what she believed was correct.

"The Twilight Hour, 'Awake Thou That Sleepest'" describes her love of meditation and reflection at dusk and tells of Mrs. Eddy calling back Calvin Frye to life when he had been carried unconscious to her.

In "Leadership and Devotion to Her Cause," Mrs. Eddy comments about the burden of responsibility for the cause and her own suffering for it.

And in "Childhood Experiences," Mrs. Eddy shares with Dickey many incidents and traits she exhibited in childhood.

That was it.

But before the book could be published, February 8, 1925, he died, and his wife saw the book through to publication.

Had he followed his leader's stated request? He let her own words—her request that he tell that she was mentally murdered—stand for that case.

Perhaps he was uncomfortable affirming mental murder as the cause of her death because he did not fully believe it. We do not know. His own reiteration of what she wished him to do, "Mother, I will do what you request of me, namely write a history of what I have seen and heard from your lips concerning your life," was not exactly what she had asked. But she had seemed satisfied with that statement, tacitly accepting what he had said he would do. Her own words, "That will do, dear," may be the best statement that can be made about his effort.

Adam Dickey's final statement about what Christian Scientists should think about the permanency of their movement appeared in the article, "The Mother Church and the Manual," in the April, 1922, *Christian Science Journal.*

The question has been asked, "Is it not strange that Mrs. Eddy put the government of The Mother Church in the hands of five persons?" Christian Scientists do not understand that she did this. What she did was to put the government of The Mother Church into the By-laws. The church is not being governed by persons; it is governed by Principle through the By-laws of the Manual. Our leader tells us that man is self-governed properly only when he is governed by God. The government of the church lies in obedience to the Manual. When the Manual is obeyed absolutely and implicitly, the church is being governed according to the law of God. When the Manual is disregarded, the church is in danger . . ..

What a wonderful organization we have, when we consider
that it is all set forth in a few simple rules that are so easy to obey
that everyone ought to be glad to give his entire and ready support to every By-law contained in the Manual . . .. It is indeed
the most simple form of church government of which the world
knows anything . . ..

And he also admonishes, "If each individual will see that he is in his
place, and standing there with God, then no attempt on the part of error
can possibly affect The Mother Church."

But Dickey had to have known that the board's jurisdiction had gone
beyond the simple formula he describes in the article. Lawsuits had affirmed
and consolidated their power, precedents were set up whereby decisions
were made at "headquarters." Procedural ways of doing things were moving
to entrench "Christian Science culture" that depended as much on custom
as on the *Manual* and theology of Christian Science. "The Mother Church
and the Manual" article may have been exhorting the board to revisit original directions.

The honesty in Dickey's book did not please the board of the Christian Science Church. When its members read the new book, the board
acted immediately.

Chapter Thirteen

Publication and Suppression

Adam Dickey was laid to rest at Mount Auburn Cemetery near the tomb of Mary Baker Eddy. A eulogizing editorial in the *Christian Science Sentinel* followed, February 21, 1925. In the editorial signed by The Christian Science Board of Directors, Dickey is called "our beloved associate and co-worker."[1] An obituary in the *Boston Herald* states:

> He was a trustee of the Mrs. Eddy estate, a member of the S.A.R. club, the Brae Burn Country Club and the Scottish Rite Masons. Mr. Dickey is survived by his widow, Mrs. Lillian S. Dickey: three sisters, the Misses Louise, Lillian and Florence and four brothers, Walter, Nathaniel, Frederick and Harold, all of Kansas City.[1]

Lillian Dickey dealt with her husband's passing courageously. She stayed close to his family, particularly to Elizabeth "Liz" Dickey, the daughter of Adam's brother Fred. Liz was sprightly and witty, and she had visited her aunt and uncle as often as possible since she was a child. "Aunt Lil was determined his book would be published, even if it wasn't finished," Elizabeth Dickey Herman has said. "And he and she fell out of favor because of it."

Lillian gathered the notes and transcriptions that constituted the book in its draft form and put them together. A July 13, 1927, order from Merrymount Press for her specifies an order for 2,000 high-quality vellum paper, hardcover books to be bound, and 3,000 more to be kept in printed sheets. Costs were $4,850, a high printer's fee that attests to the quality of photo reproduction sheets, paper, and binding. Two copies were to go to the British Museum. The others were intended for the Dickey Association members and whoever in the public at large should be interested. The printer's log lists two pickups of the book, "500 called for Oct. 5, 1927, 470 called for October 8, 1927."[2]

Dickey's pupils received copies at the association meeting October 6, buying the book from the back of the room. But the board reacted as soon as it heard about it and on December 16 sent Dickey Association members a letter. In that first letter and subsequently through several contacts with specific members they stated that they had been astonished at the contents of the book, particularly at descriptions of Mrs. Eddy's everyday life. There was in these several responses an implication that the writing sounded so unlike Adam Dickey, that they questioned whether Dickey had even written the book. Their contentions in answer to the Dickey students' inquiries about the unjustness of the ban on the book were:

- The book presented an unfair and misleading picture of Mrs. Eddy's homelife. It included trivialities and therefore subordinated the grandeur of the leader's life and message."
- It conflicted with the *Manual* because it was unjust to her.
- It would give aid and succor to the enemies of Christian Science by showing Mrs. Eddy's battles with physical disorders and might harm the faith of new students who could lose their confidence in Christian Science healing if they knew she had physical problems.
- It upheld George Glover's contention that Mrs. Eddy was obsessed with malicious animal magnetism.
- It was not a "memoir" of Mrs. Eddy because "memoir" means a person authors his or her own story.
- Mrs. Eddy probably changed her mind about Mr. Dickey's need to "write my story" because she never mentioned it again and was known to have changed her mind about biographies others suggested. He should have just written it down and deposited it in the archives

Lillian Dickey did not oppose the directors' wishes and sent her own letter to the students. They were requested to send books back to the board, which disposed of them.

The students may have complied, but for quite a while they continued to challenge the suppression. They rasied the issue that Judge Smith's mouthpiece was answering for the board. The board expanded its arguments about the suppression (they did not like that word) stating, in effect, that at the time Mrs. Eddy asked to have her secretary tell the world she died of mental murder, she was too ill to know what she was doing and probably regretted the request (though there was no evidence for this). They stood staunchly by their view that her image as a spiritual leader was demeaned by talk about her person and dress and daily habits. The veiled suggestion that Mrs. Dickey may have pushed through the project for personal reasons is there, though what those reasons might be were never explained.

As could be expected, newspapers caught the scent and had a heyday sensationalizing some of the book's descriptions. Pulitzer's *New York*

World, February 29, 1928, headlined, "Suppressed Book Tells Last Days of Mrs. M.B. Eddy" with a subhead "Bodyguard of Christian Scientists Fought Night and Day to Ward off 'Mental Assassins.'" The article emphasized the night watches as well as the raising of Calvin Frye from the dead. A copy of the book was obviously available to the *World* reporter, who reviewed its contents in detail.

As 1928 moved on, the story became the suppression as well as the truth of the stories in the book. The *World* headlined on March 1, 1928, "Eddy Book True, Says Judge Who Had It Recalled." Subheads: "C.P. Smith of Christian Science Publication committee Confirms Dickey *Memoirs* Revealed by *The World*. Backs Up The Account of Her Raising the Dead But Volume as a Whole Gives False Picture, He says; Further Extracts Presented."

Judge Smith had been a comrade-in-arms of Adam Dickey for fifteen years. The vigorous questioning of the matter by association students may be reflected by a statement in the *World*, "He denied vigorously that Mrs. Dickey had been threatened in any way." She had not lost her pension (she didn't have one). "Judge Smith appeared frankly distressed because the existence of two copies of the [book] had been discovered in the Congressional Library's Rare Book Room and reporters were now using them to excerpt its contents. He [Judge Smith] spoke continuously of persecution." The reporter summarized major sections of the book, thus thrusting its information forward in a way that might not have been tempting to newspapers except for the church's "suppression" and the committee on publication's discomfiture.

The *World* also publicized a bizarre side issue the book's publication had raised. For some time, as was mentioned earlier, Annie C. Bill had been claiming that Mrs. Eddy wished her church to be led by an individual, and that she was the person. The *World* reported that Mrs. Bill, a schismatic who believed she headed the rightful Christian Science Church, called, "The Christian Science Parent Church of Transforming Covenant," claimed that the Dickey book vindicated her stand. Because the book describes Mrs. Eddy's steadfastly leading her church until the end of her days—and wistfully saying if she could find one spiritually equipped individual, she would place him at the head of it, Bill stated her stand had been correct.

That same month *Life Magazine* opined about the book, which it did not seem to have read except through another periodical's articles. In the tongue-in-cheek, folksy style then popular, *Life* said:

> They represent Mrs. Eddy in her last years as organizing and maintaining a defense of herself against malicious mental attacks. It did not accord with her plans and expectations that she should die, but she felt that she might die from these malicious

attacks. When she did die, she believed that they were what had killed her.

Possibly she was mistaken about that and died like other people because she had got through.

They go on to spoof all spiritual healing, including that at Lourdes.

Dittemore jumped into the fray, writing a letter to the board saying that Dickey, his former fellow board member, had written the book because in Dickey's last illness he had a conversion to the idea that board rule of the church was wrong. Although, Dittemore alleged, Dickey had not listened to him during the litigation years, he saw the error of his ways as he faced death. So this book was not about Mrs. Eddy's last years, but about her distrust of board rule. What the board had really suppressed was the idea that the church should not be led by a board at all but by a person, an assertion that indirectly supported Annie Bill's case.[3]

The board had said it was "astonished" that Dickey had written the book. It had become so accustomed to controlling the "image" of Mary Baker Eddy that board members could not understand the reasons that motivated him. Those reasons should have been obvious. First, she had made him promise "before God" that he would do what she asked. Second, what he said was the truth as he knew it.

The book is not an example of literary excellence, though it is interesting to read. In addition, because it is limited in its scope, and no extensive accurate biography had been written then, there was no way an outside reader could grasp the full breadth of Mrs. Eddy's career and character by reading this little narrative. Still, it served a good purpose.

Copies became rare for the next seven decades. Any copy that could be located sold for at least $500, with the price going steadily up through the years. The name of Adam Dickey, loved secretary and confidante of Mary Baker Eddy and loyal board member for fourteen years during major growth of the Christian Science movement, faded until almost forgotten.

His two major articles, "God's Law of Adjustment" and "Possession" stayed on Reading Room shelves, but the author's name was associated with mild disfavor. It was said he had done something to discredit himself and the movement, but most could not recall what. It would take fifty years to put what Dickey had actually done for the movement into perspective.

After thirty years of distorted biographies of Mary Baker Eddy designed to blast her memory from the face of the earth, honest treatments began to appear. Robert Peel persuaded The Mother Church to allow him to use its records and told her story in three volumes in the late 1960s and 1970s. He painted a subtle but many-sided portrait. Gillian Gill's award-winning book, *Mary Baker Eddy*, took a scholarly and generally admiring look at her many-faceted life, analyzed details in other biographies and came to the conclusion that much of the negative publicity had been agenda-driven and distorted. Dickey's pictures of a woman suffering, holding up through adversity, yet triumphing in her leadership to the very end of her days were recognized as a vital part of the story and became a part of the rich weaving of threads of biography that documented her life.

Mrs. Eddy's place in American religious history began to be reevaluated in the 1980s and 1990s, as the more truthful biographies were appreciated. When impartial critics read of her life, they could understand the strains of remarkable leadership and spiritual transcendence for themselves, casting away the chaff. Both the adherent of the religion and the outsider can answer the question "Who was Mary Baker Eddy?" for him or herself.

Adam Dickey had a place in that process. Long before it was "safe" to tell the full story, one Mrs. Eddy had wanted told—suffering as well as Science—he had the courage to do it. For that, as well as being the right man at key times in the development of Christian Science, the movement and students of religious history owe him credit.

EDDY BOOK TRUE, SAYS JUDGE WHO HAD IT RECALLED

C. P. Smith of Christian Science Publication Committee Confirms Dickey Memoirs Revealed by The World

BACKS UP THE ACCOUNT OF HER RAISING THE DEAD

But Volume as a Whole Gives False Picture, He Says; Further Extracts Presented

By John E. Mitchell

Staff Correspondent of The World

BOSTON, Feb. 29.—Adam H. Dickey's account of the miraculous happenings of the last days of Mary Baker Eddy, founder of Christian Science, was officially confirmed here to-day by Judge Clifford P. Smith, Chairman of the Committee on Publication and spokesman for the Mother Church.

Judge Smith said Dickey's book represented "an honest effort" to set down the things which occurred at Mrs. Eddy's Chestnut Hill home. He confirmed specifically Dickey's account of how Mrs. Eddy "raised" her footman-secretary, Calvin A. Frye, from the dead and brought him back to life.

Denies Threats

He freely admitted that, acting as the spokesman of the Board of Directors last fall, he requested Mrs. Dickey to suppress the book, requesting all copies at the printers and recalling the copies she had sent out to Mr. Dickey's former pupils in Christian Science.

,298—DAILY. Copyright Press Publishing Company
(New York World) 1928 NEW

Suppressed Memoirs Describe Last Years Of Mary Baker Eddy

ADAM H. DICKEY.

CALVIN A. FRYE.
(From a Photograph Taken About 1882..)

Bodyguard of Christian Scientists Fought Night and Day to Ward Off "Mental Assassins".

The World is able to present the first complete eye-witness account of the days of Mary Baker Eddy, founder of Christian Science, taken from a book which the author says she specially authorized and which the regular church organization has done its utmost to suppress. It is an important document dealing with a world figure.

Also it gives a vivid account of the "death" of Calvin A. Frye, Mrs. Eddy's footman-secretary, and tells how, after a night of battling with Frye's "enemies," she raised him from the dead, and restored him to life.

1093 BEACON STREET
BROOKLINE, MASS.

October 18, 1927

Dear Friend:

The Christian Science Board
of Directors of The Mother Church, The
First Church of Christ, Scientist, in
Boston, Massachusetts, have requested
me to discontinue the publication of
the book, "Memoirs of Mary Baker Eddy"
by Adam H. Dickey, C.S.D., and to recall
all books already sold. I willingly
comply with their request.

The above will explain the
letter sent to you last week.

Very sincerely yours,

Lillian S. Dickey

The Board's Letter on Suppression of the Book

Summary of, and excerpts from, a December 16, 1927 letter from the board of the First Church of Christ, Scientist, to members of the Dickey Association.

The board begins its letter by stating they know Adam Dickey stood firmly for the movement and for Mrs. Eddy's right to privacy, often stated by her, both for herself and for her home.

That is why "Our astonishment then was great beyond expression when we read the book 'Memoirs of Mary Baker Eddy' and found it contained so much that would be harmful to make public. Neither could we really attribute its authorship to Mr. Dickey as we have known him."

The board next accuses Lillian Dickey of making a "grave mistake" in publishing a book without direct instructions from "our Leader." No one on the board, they insist, knew anything about this book until it was offered at the Association meeting.

The letter puts forth a detailed justification of the recall. "As the occasion for our action does not seem to be fully understood by some of your members, we are sending you this letter. Some of you may wonder why Mr. Dickey should do such a thing after so many years had passed since he was at our Leader's side. Others may have concluded that he could not do anything else if he were to be obedient."

But, the letter contends, there was only one occasion on which Mrs. Eddy directed Dickey to write her story. And, after all, the board tells the Association, Mrs. Eddy asked several people at various times to write her history during the latter years of her life. In at least two cases, they insist, the work was begun and was well underway when she asked that it be stopped.

The reason that the work was stopped, they say, was that she was dissatisfied with what was written. And "These writings contained nothing unjust or prejudicial to our Leader; did not disclose to the world the confidences that existed between her and those nearest to her; nor did they invade the privacy of her home which she so earnestly desired to keep inviolate. They did not include occurrences of a confidential nature in any degree comparable to the unrestrained freedom with which Mr. Dickey has recorded them."

The letter then makes veiled claims that someone else must

have written this book. Adam Dickey, the board insists, was always at Mrs. Eddy's side, protecting her from those who would intrude on her privacy. "The Adam Dickey we know" would not allow "the slightest disregard for her wishes to be left alone." And in later years, as an officer of the board and Church, Dickey had always stood firm in his "uncompromising disapproval of those who were faithless in this regard to the trust imposed in them by our Leader."

But, they wonder, how can we explain how Mrs. Eddy would ask Dickey to write her history if she did not really want it written, as they alleged? Their answer is that she asked him in a desperate moment. She was ill, "contending with an acute physical claim. She quickly recovered her physical health and mental poise, and in the two years that followed, so far as known, no mention was again made of the incident."

One request alone shouldn't count. Mrs. Eddy, they say, was always turning her household away from some particular saying she might have offered to them in the past, prayerfully revising past opinions with new insights.

Quite damning in their eyes is their belief that the book conflicts with the *Manual*. "Opinions may differ widely as to whether it is helpful or harmful, or whether its contents are accurate of exaggerated, but plainly it is unjust and therefore contrary to the *Manual*. Those who have shared our Leader's home, both before and during Mr. Dickey's residence there, unite in declaring that the book is unjust to our Leader inasmuch as it gives an unfair and misleading picture of her home life." It "gives a large place to trivialities and subordinates the grandeur of our Leader's life purpose."

Most of all the board wants to vigorously refute the view that Mrs. Eddy might have felt embattled at times, needing to defend herself against error. She could not have felt embattled, they say, because she was habitually "dwelling in the secret place of the most High and was fearless in the performance of her life work," which was destroying wickedness and bringing to mankind the Truth of Being, which could be demonstrated.

And Dickey's book was unjust because it didn't emphasize Mrs. Eddy's "transcendent wisdom, her steadfast reliance upon God, and her enduring love for her fellow man, which impelled her with infinite pains and patience to expound her discovery."

It was Article XL, Section 10 of the *Manual*, which the

board accuses Dickey of disobeying, concerning false and injurious books. The results, actually, of the publication are what make this book injurious.

They contend: all the talk about the strong attacks of mortal mind upon the household and Leader will not be understood by any but the most experienced metaphysicians. Any inspiration from the book is far outweighed by the shock most people will feel that the Leader has these human frailties.

It is particularly dismaying to the board to have Mrs. Eddy portrayed in the book as struggling against physical disorders. Newcomers to Christian Science may not be "fitted to bear" these things. Dickey should not have been instilling fear in this manner in the minds of the "timid or weak" giving them meat instead of milk, as St. Paul said and portraying struggles in the case of the Leader to those who are struggling themselves.

How the enemies of the Cause will gloat, says the letter, when they read of Mrs. Eddy's struggles.

There are other features, the letter goes on, which are offensive and constitute just cause for a recall of the book.

1. That title is inappropriate. A memoir is something that a person writes about his/her own life. It should have been called "Memoirs of Adam H. Dickey."

2. He could have fulfilled his promise if he had just written the book and "deposited the writing relating to her for preservation in the files of The Mother Church, as others of the household have considerately done."

The letter concludes with a reference by the boad (perplexing, at least in this context) from *Retrospection and Introspection*, (Page 21, line 28)

> If spiritual conclusions are separated from their premises, the nexus is lost, and the argument, with its rightful conclusions, becomes correspondingly obscure. The human history needs to be revised, and the material record expunged.

Lucie C. Warren signs the letter on behalf of The Christian Science Board of Directors.

The gang's all here! Or at least a good many of the household staff, the "family" of Mary Baker Eddy in spring or summer of 1908 at Chestnut Hill. (l to r) Alice Peck; A. McLellan; E. Kelly; I.C. Tomlinson; Nellie Eveleth; Katherine Retterer; Adam Dickey; Jonathan Irving; F. Thatcher; Adelaide Still; Margaret McDonald; Minnie Scott and Adolph Stevenson. From an original photographer's mounted portrait retained by Dickey as a memento of his remarkable time with the Discoverer and Founder of Christian Science and her loyal students.

Bibliography for Mr. *Dickey*:
Frequently used books with short titles used in the book and notes

Bates and Dittemore   Ernest Sutherland Bates and John V. Dittemore. *Mary Baker Eddy: The Truth and the Tradi-
tion*. New York: Knopf, 1932.

Beasley   Norman Beasley. *The Continuing Spirit*. New
York: Duell, Sloan and Pearce, 1956.

Dickey A. *Memoirs*   Adam Dickey, C.S.D. *Memoirs of Mary Baker
Eddy*. Brookline, Mass.: Lillian S. Dickey, C.S.B.,
1927.

Dittemore papers: Assorted papers of John V. Dittemore in the
Keith McNeil collection.

Eddy, Mary Baker   Latest editions of *Science and Health with Key to
the Scriptures, The First Church of Christ, Scientist,
and Miscellany*, and *The Manual of The Mother
Church, The First Church of Christ, Scientist in Boston, Mass*.

Frye diary   Diary of Calvin Frye in the Mary Baker Eddy Library for the Betterment of Humanity on CD.

Gill   Gillian Gill. *Mary Baker Eddy*. Cambridge Biography Series, Cambridge, Massachusetts: Per-
seus Books, 1998.

Peel   Robert Peel. *Mary Baker Eddy* 3 vols. New York:
Holt, Rinehart and Winston. *The Years of Discovery, 1966. The Years of Trial, 1971. The Years
of Authority, 1977*.

Rathvon diary   The unpublished diary of William Rathvon in
the Mary Baker Eddy Library for the Betterment
of Humanity.

Other books:

Dickey, Kenneth McM. *A Man With Clay Feet*. Kansas City: Mount Forest
Press, 1953.

Martin V. Melosi. *The Sanitary City: Urban Infrastructure in America from Colonial Times to the Present*. Baltimore and London: Johns Hopkins University Press, 2000.

Notes

Chapter One

1. The Elizabeth Dickey Herman collection forms the basis of information in this book on early family experiences of Adam Dickey. Letters, photos, journal entries, and genealogical information in this chapter are from that collection.

"Liz" Herman, the daughter of Adam's brother Fred, was the niece of Adam and Lillian Dickey. She inherited a sizeable collection of items from the Longyear Estate home of the Dickeys, family records, mementos, and documents from the time of the Irish ancestors through the years Adam Dickey spent with Mary Baker Eddy. Elizabeth Dickey Herman died in February, 2005. Both she and her daughter Nancie Callender Baxter had long shared stories of Dickey and the collection with me, knowing I was a Christian Scientist. Although the mother and daughter had no interest in Christian Science, they were very interested in having his story told.

Dickey wrote of his family's religious tradition in the preface to his *Memoirs of Mary Baker Eddy* and in other documents shared with his Christian Science association and students from time to time. Those written traditions about the family life he and Lillian shared with the association are now in the archives at the Mary Baker Eddy Library for the Betterment of Humanity.

The Longyear Foundation has other documents about his life. Of particular interest is the "Quarterly News of the Mary Baker Eddy Museum and Historic Sites," published by Longyear Historical Society, Spring, 1974, which pulls together several pieces of information in their files. The article is by Anne Holiday Webb.

I have cited identifying information on specific documents from the family collection in the text itself.

Chapter Two

1. Kenneth McMullen Dickey's small booklet about his father, *A Man with Clay Feet*, is both helpful and puzzling. The book is detailed and intelligently written and follows the development of Kansas City Sewer Pipe, later W. S Dickey Clay Manufacturing Company, through its several stages. I have depended on this account along with the business records at the Kansas City Public Library. The tone of bitter recrimination—a son writing negatively about a father—makes the reader uncomfortable. Still, the career of Walter Dickey is a morality play, even taken at its literal level. We see a man dominated by the drive to succeed. His last venture of buying newspapers and combining them to provide a strong political presence in the city ended in

the loss of his own fortune. His family has the tradition that when Walter Dickey died, he did not have enough money to pay for his tombstone.

2. The Kansas City Public Library website provides information on Dickey clay pipe industries.

Chapter Three

1. *The Christian Science Journal* listed services around the country in the early 1890s, many of them in storefronts or assembly halls, often with "speakers."

The first services in Kansas City, according to *Journals* of the period, were held in two locations. Emma Behan of the "Missouri Christian Science Institute" was the "speaker." The small group sponsored both morning and afternoon church services.

2. Adam Dickey and his wife told the story of their early conversion to Christian Science, class instruction, and service to the church in Kansas City to the Dickey Association. These records are in the Mary Baker Eddy Library HF Dickey file collection. Box 39 contains many of the papers and recollections donated to the archives. Dickey's original membership booklet on joining The Mother Church is in the collection of Keith McNeil, Petaluma, California.

3. The church burned in 1910 and was rebuilt almost immediately. First Church of Christ, Scientist, Kansas City, on dissolution, sent its records to the Mary Baker Eddy Library.

4. The description of the Communion Season of 1897 has been one of the best loved and often told in the lore of Christian Science. Robert Peel describes it in *Mary Baker Eddy: The Years of Authority*, pp.108-110.

5. Peel describes the lecture in Kansas City as a particularly striking one in *The Years of Authority*, p. 123. The relationship of the Kimballs and Mrs. Eddy is one of rare friendship in her life. More light is thrown on Kimball's contributions in *The Years of Authority*, pp. 190-193.

6. The *World* article was supplied by Longyear Museum.

7. Dickey describes the Mexico City episode himself and other incidents in his life as a Christian Scientist at this time, in the HF Dickey file collection in the Mary Baker Eddy Library.

Chapter Four

1. Peel, *The Years of Authority*, p. 247. Gillian Gill spends a good deal of time discussing the household situation and those in it, pp. 399-408. She deals with the wariness and somberness of the staff. Particularly interesting is her refutation of the claims that Mrs. Eddy was fixated on neatness. Gill contends that Victorian women were brought up to value household cleanliness and neatness above many other virtues, and that it was a given that neat dress and housekeeping were marks of character. Understanding this,

it is possible to see that Mrs. Eddy was not only trying to demonstrate the perfection of detail that should be part of true personhood, but was also a child of her age.

2. The sunset glory quotation is in Peel, *The Years of Authority*, p. 113, cited as L&M 88-12999; the "patching breaches" quotation is from *Mis.*, p. 316.

3. Peel covers the Julia Field-King matter in *The Years of Authority*, p. 116, and the Clara Choate matter's climax in *The Years of Trial*, pp. 145, 146.

4. Peel: *The Years of Trial*, p. 155.

5. Gestefeld is discussed in Peel: *The Years of Trial*, pp. 231-235.

Chapter Five

1. John V. Dittemore, who was on the board with Dickey, described him as a "bull-necked Canadian with the face of a prize-fighter" and an "athletic tiger cat." Quoted by Gill, p. 527, from Bates-Dittemore. This may or may not have been how the family at Chestnut Hill saw him. Certainly he was known for decisiveness. Gill describes Dittemore as "a rival" of Dickey. Dickey was naturalized in 1887.

2. Mary Baker Eddy Library, L07009.

3. Peel: *The Years of Authority*, p. 297, citing a letter to Alfred Farlow L&M 14-1719.

4. The Mary Baker Eddy Library believes that Arthur Reeves Vosburg served as Mrs. Eddy's secretary January and February, 1908. Vosburg, however, came a little later than Dickey's recorded arrival at the house, so the unidentified secretary may have been John Lathrop, if Lathrop was not the earlier visitor.

5. "Working for the weather" apparently meant praying for harmony in the weather—against extreme conditions.

6. Dittemore's views of Dickey, which went through several stages, are expressed in the book he co-authored with Bates in 1932.

Chapter Six

1. Peel:*The Years of Authority*: "Entrenched materialism," p. 172; "Mrs. Eddy's equivalent of original sin," pp. 67.

2. Peel reports the newspaper article by Reverend Adams in *The Years of Trial*, p. 265.

3. Peel: Annie Dodge letter in *The Years of Authority*, p. 298. His chapter IX notes cite L&M 91-13479.

4. Document in the HF Dickey file collection, Mary Baker Eddy Library.

5. The note is used courtesy of the Mary Baker Eddy collection. It is in the Mary Baker Eddy Library, Document 103873.

6. Peel: *The Years of Authority*, p. 315.

7. The box containing Dickey's journal notes was reviewed by this author in 1987. That part of the Elizabeth Dickey Herman collection was sold and remained in private hands for twenty years. In 2007 Keith McNeil obtained the collection and it was thus made available to the public through this book's new edition. It adds a good deal of original material about the period including the fact that Dickey approved of founding *The Monitor*.

8. Frye diary for July 2, 1908.

9. Rathvon's diary used through the courtesy of the Mary Baker Eddy Collection.

Chapter Seven

1. *My*, p. 358.

2. Rathvon diary, December 15, 1909.

3. Bates-Dittemore, pp. 447-448.

4. Her notice in the *Sentinel* is noted in *The Years of Authority*, p. 345; citing CSS, XII 20. The quotation about organization is from the same book, p. 346 which cites Smith in *The Permanency of The Mother Church and Its Manual* published by the Christian Science Publishing Society, 1954, p. 10. Peel is also the source for the discussion in this section on "the succession."

5. The letter of Rathvon, Judge Smith, and Judge Hanna is labeled, "Exhibit A Rathvon to Dickey," in the Mary Baker Eddy Library, HF Dickey file collection.

6. The prayer was a gift to the historical department of The Mother Church by Florence Dickey in 1935 and is now part of the HF Dickey file collection. Courtesy Mary Baker Eddy Collection.

7. Gill presents a full picture of the last period of Mrs. Eddy's Life in *Mary Baker Eddy*. Her discussion of the attempt to settle with Glover is p. 543; Gill's material on the morphine problem has largely been based on Frye's diary entries. In 1906 it reported Dr. Morrill's administering from 1/8 to ¼ grain of morphine by hypodermic with specific instructions for giving repeated doses if necessary. Historians have found several other documented uses of Mrs. Eddy's using morphine for intense "renal pain." Edwin Franden Dakin first reported the use of the drug to the general public.

The leader's frailty in her latter days and passing is summarized well in Gill, pp. 547-549.

8. The "other side" letter to "Miss [not named] was dated Chestnut Hill, Oct 25, 1908, [crossed out and in handwriting, 1909] and received by The Mother Church from [in handwriting] "Marion May, N.Y. and Mrs. Veassey, Chicago," July, 1941. HF Dickey file collection at the Mary Baker Eddy Library.

9. *Quarterly News*, Longyear Historical Society, Spring, 1974.

10. A copy of a series of excerpts of letters from Adam Dickey to Ula Olldenburg, May 27, 1913, supplied to the author by Manfred Soellinger, Essen, Germany.

11. The digest of Dickey entries in Calvin Frye's diary was summarized by Keith McNeil and the enties are used through the courtesy of the Mary Baker Eddy collection. Original, non-standardized punctuation has been retained. Frye emphasizes "time off" and personal obligations for which Dickey received permission from Mrs. Eddy. He himself had had virtually no time off since he came to work for his leader.

Chapter Eight

1. Much of the specific material from this chapter about the actual functioning of the Board of Directors of The Mother Church procedurally and in the legal cases comes from Norman Beasley's *The Continuing Spirit*. Beasley searched original sources. Changes in board membership, statistics on the growth of The Mother Church, and quotations on the dismissal of Dittemore are from Beasley.

2. *Christian Science Sentinel*, December 16, 1916.

3. The discussion of the lawsuits begins on pp. 40-44 in Beasley.

4. Charles Braden, *Christian Science Today*. Dallas: Southern Methodist University Press, 1961, p. 381, is one source.

5.The legal proceedings involving these two branches of authority in the Church of Christ, Scientist, are recorded in the ponderous volume titled *Proceedings in Equity* available at the Mary Baker Eddy Library and a few other depositories. *Proceedings in Equity*, pp. 735-739, introduces the salary controversy. Testimony in court during the litigation shows board members were receiving $10,000 per year at that time.

6. William McCrackan was a trusted associate editor of the *Christian Science Sentinel*, who later ran afoul of the board in the litigation controversy. His typescript states he is trying to deal fairly with Adam Dickey, who was a fellow classmate of his in a class taught by Edward Kimball. He knew Adam Dickey over a long period of time. A careful reading shows he was a supporter of John Dittemore and probably Annie Bill. His comments in the document, that there were too many "stocky men" in positions of power and that Dickey was too fat, show the later hostility that developed between the two men. What physical weight or appearance had to do with administrational capability, especially for people who were trying to see the spiritual self, is not clear. The Edwardian ideal of handsome manhood, however, was a slim and not-too-tall figure with a goatee and dapper manners. That was not Dickey. The pyramid furor is discussed in this document in the Dickey file collection at the Mary Baker Eddy Library. Andrew Hartsook also discussed it in *Christian Science after 1910*, Zanesville, Ohio, 1993, quoting from the *Washington Newsletters* p. 20.

Chapter Nine

1. The story of the remarkable service of Christian Scientists to their fellow men and women in World War I was published by The Christian Science Publishing Society as *Christian Science War Time Activities*, 1922. It is out of print today.

2. One of the sources for stories of Adelaide Still in this book is Denis Glover of Chatham, Massachusetts, the editor of this book, who as a young man interviewed Still.

3. Andrew Hartsook, citing p. 24 from *The Alice Orgain Letters* pp. 99, 100-102.

Chapter Ten

1. John Dittemore papers, letter of May 28, 1919, Keith McNeil Collection.

2. I have relied heavily on Beasley's summary of the litigation and on the John Dittemore papers in the collection of Keith McNeil.

3. The *Boston Globe* article is in the collection of the Longyear Museum. "Bill of Complaint," filed April 29, 1919, and "Answer of Adam H. Dickey, James A. Neal, Edward A. Merritt and William R. Rathvon to Complaint of John V. Dittemore" are both from the Dittemore collection of Keith McNeil.

4 Ann Holiday Webb, *Longyear Quarterly News*, Longyear Historical Society, Spring 1974.

5. Beasley, p. 180.

Chapter Eleven

1. Ornamental Chinese jars and woodwork from the Dickey "Chinese room" are in the home of Nancie Callender Baxter, his grand-niece. The article about the house is from the Keith McNeil Collection.

2. HF Dickey file collection, Mary Baker Eddy Library.

3. "Treatment" is in the HF Dickey file used courtesy of the Mary Baker Eddy Collection. Folder titled "Address and Papers" with the handwritten notation at the top, "Received from Miss Florence Dickey, February 15, 1935."

Chapter Twelve

1. The copy of *Memoirs of Mary Baker Eddy* cited in this book and reproduced at its end belongs to the Dickey family and is one of the few books kept back during the suppression.

Chapter Thirteen

1. The *Boston Herald* obituary from the Keith McNeil Collection, February 9, 1925. All newspaper editorials, commentaries, and articles in this

chapter are from this collection, either as originals or copies, unless other-wise noted.

2. Five-hundred copies were originally delivered and accounted for, not the 2,000 contracted for. Most of the 500 were destroyed at the request of The Mother Church board. But the second 470 are unaccounted for. They were probably destroyed, along with the "printed sheets" not bound at the time of delivery.

3. A copy of the open Dittemore letter to the board is in the Keith McNeil Collection.

About the Author

Nancy Niblack Baxter is the author of nine books on nineteenth century America and taught high school and college English and history for twenty-three years. She was awarded the Eli Lilly Lifetime Achievement Award in History from the Indiana Historical Society in 2000. A wife, mother, grandmother, and avid gardener, she lives in Carmel, Indiana.

From: www.amazon.com

Non-fiction
Gallant Fourteenth: The Story of an Indiana Civil War Regiment
The Miamis!
Hoosier Farmboy in Lincoln's Army

Fiction:
The Heartland Chronicles
The Movers: A Saga of the Scotch Irish
Lords of the Rivers
The Dream Divided: Indiana in the Civil War
All The Bright Sons of Morning
Charmed Circle

On Christian Science:
From Hawthorne Publishing, 15601 Oak Road, Carmel, IN 46033
www.hawthornepub.com or www.amazon.com
Open the Doors of the Temple: The Survival of Christian Science in the Twenty First Century

Nancy Baxter is member of The Mother Church, The First Church of Christ, Scientist, in Boston, Massachusetts, and has held memership in various branch churches around the country for fifty years.

A Chestnut Hill

Album

Mrs. Eddy presented this image of herself as a woman in mid-life to Adam Dickey. Un-less otherwise indicated, all photographs in this album are from Adam and Lillian Dickey's private Chestnut Hill collection owned by Elizabeth Dickey Herman and obtained by Keith McNeil, or from his general collection of records of the Christian Science movement.

Introduction

In August 1909 Mary Baker Eddy told her secretary, Adam Dickey, "God is preparing a history for you, and you are writing it now." In his journal entries he noted that she meant "My daily life and experience here [at Chestnut Hill] is the history."

This *Chestnut Hill Album* of journal entries and photographs documents the history that Dickey, as well as his spiritual leader and admired friend, Mrs. Eddy, and other members of her household, were leading 1908-1910, the years when Christian Science had reached an early pinnacle of success and fulfillment.

When my first edition of *Mr. Dickey* came out in 2005 based on available research materials, it concluded with Dickey's *Memoirs of Mary Baker Eddy*, a book which up to that time was exeedingly rare, with only a few original copies extant in the United States. As a result of that republication of the *Memoirs,* thousands of interested people have been able to read this book in its original format.

The *Memoirs* was made available to the author by Elizabeth Dickey Herman and her daughter Nancie. Elizabeth was the daughter of Adam Dickey's brother Fred and became Adam and Lillian Dickey's heir. Elizabeth had sold Dickey's journals and some other papers to a collector in 1988, retaining many historical records of the Dickey family for herself. These retained records formed the basis of the biographical material on Dickey which is the first part of this book.

Since the publication of the first edition, the journals of Adam Dickey have come to light again, recently acquired by one of the leading historians of the Christian Science movement, Keith McNeil. Through Keith's conviction that historical records are important to understanding Christian Science, these new journal entries and photographic images collected by Adam Dickey from his years at Chestnut Hill have been made available to readers for this album. The story of Chestnut Hill during Mrs. Eddy's last three years, then, replaces the *Memoirs* in this edition.

Mrs. Eddy's trust in her assistant Adam Dickey was deep and abiding. She believed he had thoroughly absorbed her teaching that God is all there is to existence in the spiritual universe, that the full and Christly understanding of man's true nature heals and transforms all of life.

Mrs. Eddy particularly trusted him to transmit her conviction that

Christianity is both a crown and a cross lived in daily life. This collection shows that nothing meant more to her in her later years than having her students understand that the agonizing challenges that had come to both the Master and herself as founder of Christian Science would have to be shared in some degree by their followers. The triumph of Christian Science would not be won through a path of flowers.

To see this intimate portrait of one of the great women in American history in its entirety is to see her fidelity to her vision, her trust in God, and her perceptive leadership of her church until the last of her earthly life, even through difficult times.

Adam Dickey did not write his daily record in Mrs. Eddy's household in a neat, daily journal. Some days he wrote, other days, when he was occupied with his job, probably not. His daily jottings were invariably down-to-earth and unvarnished. He recorded Bible lessons Mrs. Eddy conducted every day when she gathered her household. But he also wrote of staff bickering, reprimands over food, comings and goings of church officers, and the personal struggles of the staff to satisfy the many needs of the leader while having some life of their own. Most of the household "family" simply gave up the desire for some normal life. Dickey did not, insisting his wife be near him. Bringing that matter to a head with his employer, whom he deeply loved, must have been one of the hardest things in his life, but the way he handled the situation is a mark of the directness he usually had when dealing with Mrs. Eddy.

In addition to the daily notations and descriptions he left, he also had his wife retain his letters. Many years later he put diary entries and letters together to write the *Memoirs of Mary Baker Eddy*. But much did not get included in that book. These newly available documents go far beyond what the *Memoirs* was able to record in terms of daily life and the leader's metaphysical messages to her staff. They are thus a fresh and original treasure for both historians and dedicated students of Chrsistian Science.

The journal entries are actually transcripts, copies. The handwriting is that of Lillian Dickey, Adam's wife, who lived a part of this history at Chestnut Hill. Her husband's originals no longer exist, possibly disposed of because of the difficulties with the directors, who opposed Dickey's publication of his *Memoirs*.

Lillian aided him in preparing the book and organized the Chestnut Hill records, transcribing his scribbles into coherent entries.

It is obvious that there were more entries than these surviving ones, but they were not in the collection as it came to his heirs. There are no entries for 1910; we can surmise that they did exist at one time. Although we are thankful for what we have, since these segments are so interesting, we wonder what the 1910 group would have contained. The "notes" (typed by Dickey or another transcriber) at the end of this collection suggest unexplored and intriguing memories of those years we will probably never have.

I have included both images of original journal pages and my own transcriptions. I have italicized Mrs. Eddy's words, thus eliminating the inconsistent quotation marks which appear in the originals,but have left consistent misspellings as they were. (Adam/Lillian spelled Archibald McLellan's name in diferent ways. The word "lightning" was misspelled.) Taken with the photos which the Dickeys snapped with their Kodak box camera, these vignettes form a charming and vivid picture of life in a remarkable, historic household one hundred years ago.

My thanks to the permissions department of the Mary Baker Eddy Collection, particularly Sally Ulrich, who worked through complicated "rights" issues for several months to be able to give Hawthorne Publishing the ability to publish several photos.

Appreciation is also offered to the great and dedicated professionals of the Mary Baker Eddy Library who researched those complicated issues.

In 2008, the year of the 100th anniversary of Adam Dickey's arrival at Chestnut Hill.

Nancy Niblack Baxter

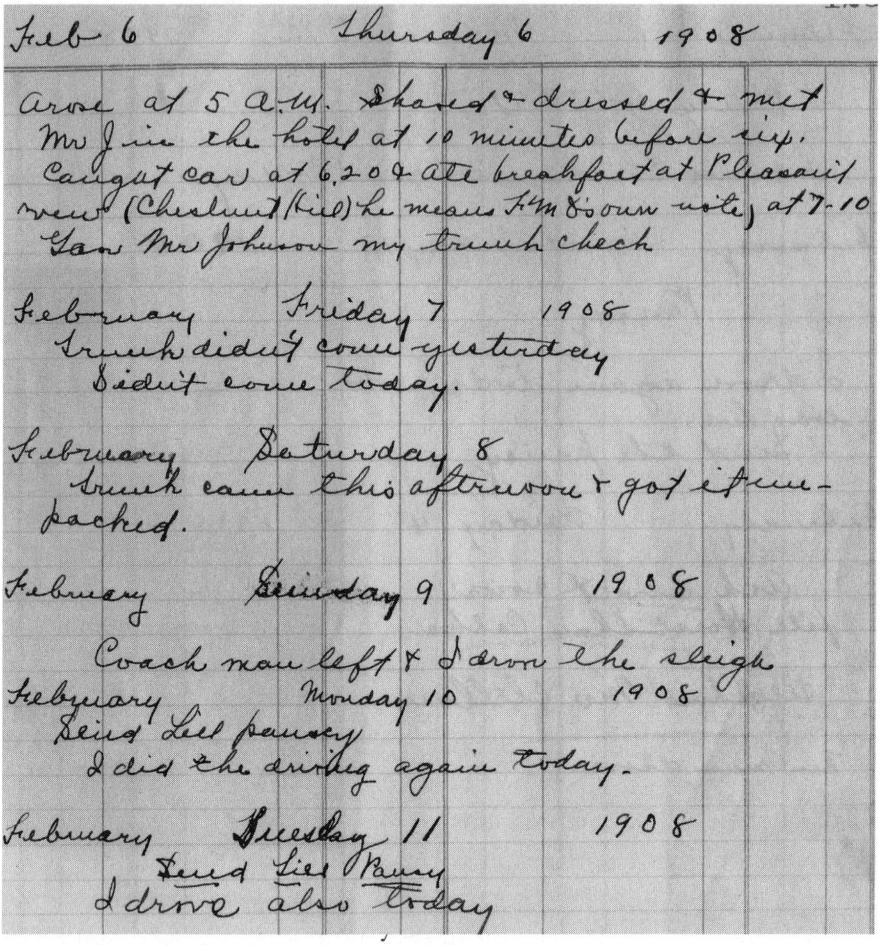
Feb 6 Thursday 6 1908
Arose at 5 A.M. Shaved & dressed & met
Mr J in the hotel at 10 minutes before six.
Caught car at 6.20 & ate breakfast at Pleasant
View (Chestnut Hill) he means L.M.D's own note) at 7-10
Gave Mr Johnson my trunk check

February Friday 7 1908
Trunk didn't come yesterday
Didn't come today.

February Saturday 8
Trunk came this afternoon & got it unpacked.

February Sunday 9 1908

Coach man left & I drove the sleigh
February Monday 10 1908
Send Lil pansy
I did the driving again today.

February Tuesday 11 1908
Send Lil Pansy
I drove also today

Arose at 5 a.m. Shaved & dressed & met Mr. J* in the hotel at 10 minutes before six.
Caught car at 6.20 & ate breakfast at Pleasant View (Chestnut Hill he means LMD's own note) at 7.10
Gave Mr. Johnson my trunk check

February Friday 7 1908
Trunk didn't come yesterday.
Didn't come today.

February Saturday 8
Trunk came this afternoon & got it unpacked.

* Mr. William B. Johnson, Clerk of The Mother Church.

February Sunday 9 1908
Coach man left & I drove the sleigh

February Monday 10 1908
Send Lill pansy_
I did the driving again today.

February Tuesday 11 1908
<u>Send</u> <u>Lill</u> <u>pansy</u>
I drove also today.

Snow at Chestnut Hill with pine trees. Mrs. Eddy believed heavy snow in a lo-
cale around any home was not harmonious, and prayerful work should keep it from
disturbing home life. Dickey first encountered her views on snow when he arrived in
1908.

February   Wednesday 12   1908
Pansy for Lill
I drove the horses again today.

February   Thursday 13   1908
Pansy
I drove again today - but new man was here.
Sent the pansy.

February   Friday 14   1908
Ask <u>about</u> course.
Fill <u>Horse Shoe</u> <u>Calks</u>
Telephone Mc Clellan
New man drove.

The garden at Chestnut Hill in winter. Formal beds and a grape arbor show careful Edwardian gardening practices.

February   Tuesday 18   1908
page 1   p. 18   as Ad has it.

Never fear a lie – declare against it with the consciousness of its nothingness. Throw your whole weight into the right scale. This is the way to destroy evil. Never weight against ourselves by admitting a lie.

February   Wednesday 19   1908
    All in - walked over & sat down. What have you to say to me this morning? & c.
    I shall stop talking evil or about it. Shall talk nothing but good - there is nothing else.

Up 1.30 a.m. til 2.30

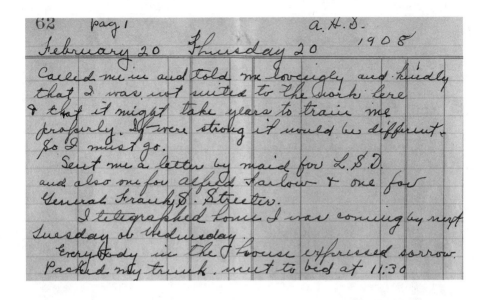

February 20   Thursday 20   1908

Called me in and told me lovingly and kindly that I was not suited to the work here & that it might take years to train me properly. If —were strong it would be different. So I must go.

Sent me a letter by maid for L.S.D. and also one for Alfred Farlow & one for General Frank S. Streeter.

I telegraphed home I was coming by next Tuesday or Wednesday.

Everyone in the house expressed sorrow. Packed my trunk, went to bed at 11:30

Front gate leading into Chestnut Hill.

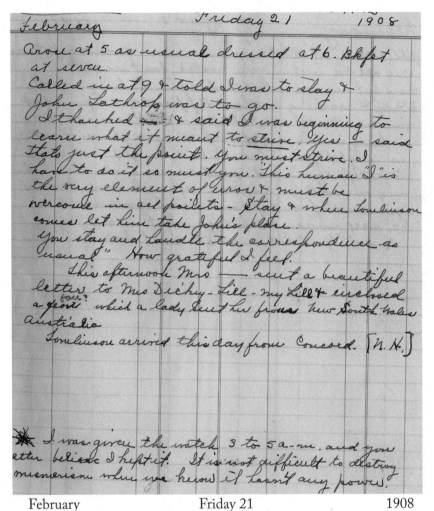

February   Friday 21   1908

Arose at 5 as usual dressed at 6. Bkfst at seven. Called in at 9 & told I was to stay & John Lathrop was to go.

I thanked [MBE]& said I was beginning to learn what it meant to <u>strive</u>. *Yes – said that's just the point. You must strive. I have to do it so must you. This human "I" is the very element of error & must be overcome in all points – Stay & when Tomlinson comes let him take John's place.*

You stay and handle the correspondence as usual. How grateful I feel.

This afternoon Mrs—[MBE] sent a beautiful letter to Mrs. Dickey - Lill - my Lill & enclosed a [illegible] which a lady sent her from New South Wales Australia.

Tomlinson arrived this day from Concord. [N.H.]

*I was given the watch 3 to 5 a.m. and you better believe I kept it. It is not difficult to destroy mesmerism when we know it hasn't any power.

Rear balcony at Chestnut Hill. Standing seem to be Dickey, Laura Sargent and possibly Calvin Frye.

February	Saturday 22	1908
11-1	11-1	
2-4	1-3	
5-7	3-5	
	5-7	
Recalled 1	watch	
" 2	hearing & sight	

February   Sunday 23   1908

John Lathrop left this morning for New York.

February   Monday 24   1908

All called at 8:20 a.m. in new rooms upstairs. *You all did well in your watch last night. Now let us see what God says* - taking up the Bible and reading without difficulty - opened at random Matt 24 -41 to 43 – Told us about waking in the night & spilling a glass of water so night gown had to be changed, but went to sleep again all night showing we were keeping our watch. I spoke up and said, "Mother you said if we kept our watch you would be a well woman & that is what we are trying to do" *Yes that is what must be.*

Dickey (r) and others, all likely to be from the household, at study table.

February Teach/ Tuesday 25 ✓ 1908

Called everybody at 8.20 a.m. and asked us all to take
our thought off her directly.
Told to declare the power presence & omnipotence of
God. If God is all there is nothing to deny but all is.
You would not say to a child—you are small you
you are young you are little. No. You would let God
take care of that, wouldn't you?—Do you see what I
mean? Now there is nothing but God & what God
creates. Can't you all see that? Isn't the Truth
declared a denial of error? If that which claimed to
cause man's downfall had never appeared in world all be
in heaven now wouldn't we?—Then bringing that which
is true & real into consciousness will destroy that which
is false and unreal won't it?
I cannot go back on Science & Health because God wrote it,
Science & Health says the lie must be counteracted, but we can
do this sometimes by knowing the allness of God. Opened the
the Bible at the last verse of the last chapter of John.
Called again at 9.00 — how God made me the way shown
didn't He?. Yes. Now S & H is showing you the way & also showing me
the way. I am meeting the claims of old age and you are &
now I have to go back to the book and learn my way from
that just as you and everybody else do. I have helped others
& now you are helping me. I have had to know that I cannot suffer because of helping others & you must know it too — be
strong on that point.

February   Teaching Tuesday 25   1908

Called everybody at 8:20 a.m. and asked us all to take our thought off
her directly.

Told to declare the power presence & omnipotence of God. If God is
all there is nothing to deny but all is.

You would not say to a child - You are small you are young you are little. No.
You would let God take care of that wouldn't you? – Do you see what I mean?
Now there is nothing but God & what God creates. Can't you all see that?
Isn't the Truth declared a denial of error? If that which claimed to cause man's
downfall had never appeared we would all be in heaven now wouldn't we?

Then bringing that which is true & real into consciousness will destroy that which is false and unreal won't it?

I cannot go back on Science & Health because God wrote it & Science & Health says the lie must counteracted, but we can do this sometimes by knowing the allness of God. Opened the Bible at the last verse of the last chapter of John.

Called again at 9:00 – *Now God made me the way shower didn't He?* Yes. *Now* S&H *is showing you the way & is also showing me the way. I am meeting the claims of old age and you are & now I have to go back to the book and learn my way from that just as you and every body else do. I have helped others & now you are helping me. I have had to know that I cannot suffer because of helping others & you must know it too – be strong on that point.*

Adam Dickey's room. Note the radiator, as the fireplaces probably were not used.

~~February~~ March Tuesday 3 1908
All called – said to Tomlinson – "You sent me in
a newspaper clipping a while ago about a woman
nearly 100 years of age who was able to be about her
house ect, and you thought that would encourage me.
but it doesn't, not one particle. There is no similarity
between her case & mine. No more than there is between
addition & subtraction, not one bit. My case is altogether
different. I am not struggling with old age but with
mesmerism & nothing but mesmerism. If I could
meet this mesmerism I would be as young & strong
as I was 40 years ago. Now go to work all of you and
destroy this mesmerism

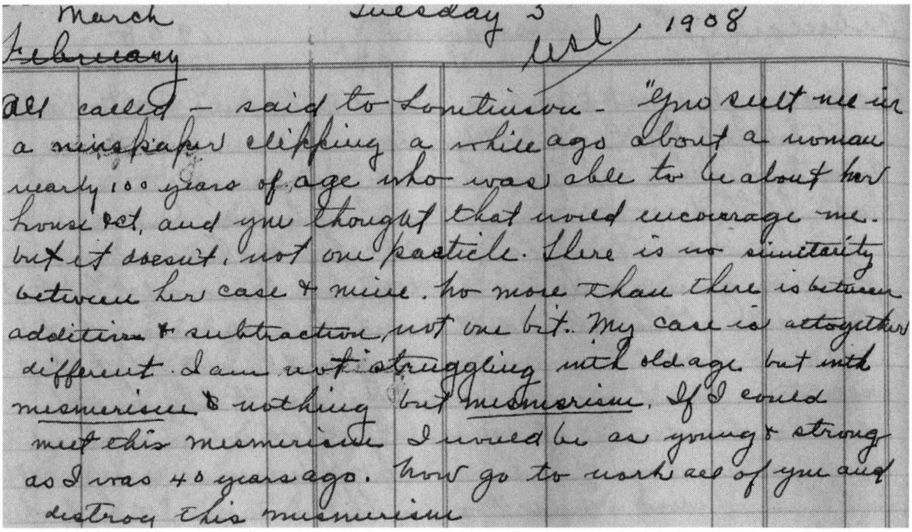

March Tuesday 3 1908

All called - said to Tomlinson-*You sent me in a newspaper clipping a while ago about a woman nearly 100 years of age who was able to be about her house ect, and you thought that that would encourage me, but it doesn't, not one particle. There is no similarity between her case & mine. No more than there is between addition and subtraction, not one bit. My case is altogether different. I am not struggling with old age but with mesmerism & nothing but mesmerism. If I could meet this mesmerism, I would be as young & strong as I was 40 years ago. Now go to work all of you and destroy this mesmerism.*

March Wednesday 4 1908
Called me & asked me to treat Laura Sargent.
said she was so disagreeable nobody could get along
with her. I went to work for her. Afterwards Mrs S.
came to my room & told me a sorrowful tale ect. &
asked me to help her. I gave her a good long talk
& she cheered up wonderfully.

March Wednesday 4 1908

Called me & asked me to treat Laura Sargent. Said she was so disagreeable nobody could get along with her. I went to work for her. Afterwards Mrs. S. came to my room & told me a sorrowful tale ect. & asked me to help her. I gave her a good long talk & she cheered up wonderfully.

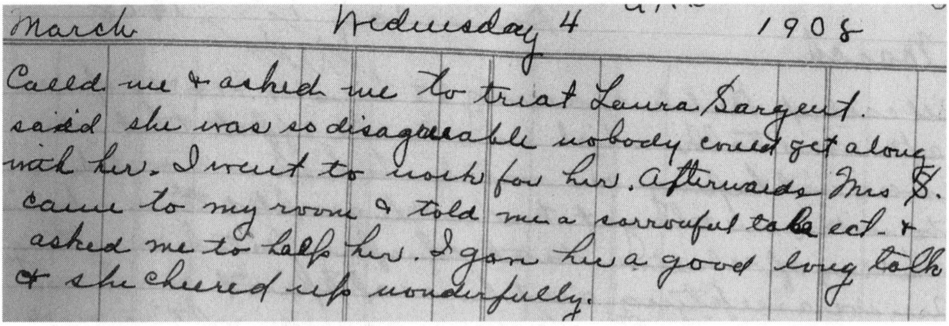

Several wings comprised the estate known as Chestnut Hill.

All called—Bible reading II [Timothy] Lines 4-14 & 15 opened after our talk which was to the effect that we were not keeping our watch. *To keep watch is to watch our thought. Now is the accepted time—now is the day of salvation. Watch therefore - Watch everything. Are we accepting as the real Spirit or matter.* I answered spirit - *Wrong! we are accepting matter.* Illustrates by balancing pencil on her finger & said *We are perfectly poised or else we are down on one side. Now toward which side are we leaning?*

I shall not ask you any more – you must answer to God – daily – hourly answer to God -

The Bible reading was about Alexander the coppersmith. *The material worker. You and Alexander the coppersmith are enemies. Look out for Alexander the Coppersmith.*

Again changed S&H page 442 about MAM asleep or awake – This is more scientifically put.

A view of the surrounding estates is shown in this photo taken from a height probably at Chestnut Hill.

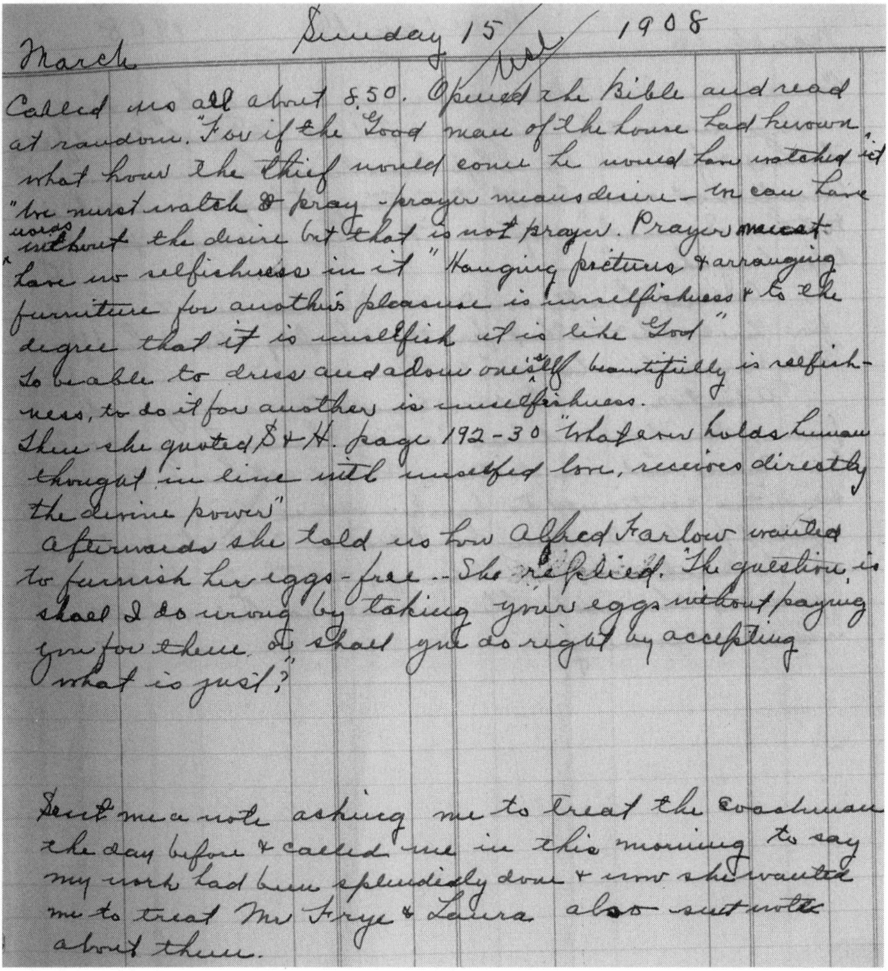
March Sunday 15 Wed 1908

Called us all about 8.50. Opened the Bible and read at random. "For if the Good man of the house had known what hour the thief would come he would have watched" etc "We must watch & pray - prayer means desire - we can have words without the desire but that is not prayer. Prayer must have no selfishness in it" Hanging pictures & arranging furniture for another's pleasure is unselfishness & to the degree that it is unselfish it is like God" To be able to dress and adorn oneself beautifully is selfishness, to do it for another is unselfishness.

Then she quoted S&H. page 192-30 "Whatever holds human thought in line with unselfed love, receives directly the divine power"

afterwards she told us how Alfred Farlow wanted to furnish her eggs - free -- She replied. The question is shall I do wrong by taking your eggs without paying you for them, or shall you do right by accepting what is just?

Sent me a note asking me to treat the coachman the day before & called me in this morning to say my work had been splendidly done & now she wanted me to treat Mr Frye & Laura also sent note about them.

March Sunday 15 1908

Called us all about 8.50. Opened the Bible and read at random. "For if the Good man of the house had known what hour the thief would come he would have watched" etc. *We must watch & pray – prayer means desire – we can have words without the desire but that is not prayer. Prayer must have no selfishness in it. Hanging pictures & arranging furniture for another's pleasure is unselfishness & to the degree that it is unselfish it is like God. To be able to dress and adorn oneself beautifully is selfishness, to do it for another is unselfishness.*

Then she quoted S&H page 192-30 "Whatever holds human thought in line with unselfed love, receives directly the divine power."

Afterwards she told us how Alfred Farlow wanted to furnish her eggs - free. She replied, *The question is shall I do wrong by taking your eggs without paying you for them, or shall you do right by accepting what is just?*

Sent me a note asking me to treat the coachman the day before & called me in the morning to say my work had been splendidly done & now she wanted me to treat Mr. Frye & Laura also sent note about them.

Adam Dickey in his bedroom at Chestnut Hill. His study books are on a little desk. Is that the "lion of Judah" which Mrs. Eddy connected with moral courage, on the wall? And near the fireplace must be the trunk that was late in arriving.

March 16   Monday   1908

Called me in the morning to say Frye had acted worse the night before & talked dreadfully to her & for me to stop treating him.

Cautioned me about treating people unasked & that I must *only do it when called upon by the wayshower.*

Called Tomlinson & me & asked me to send for her cook & talked pretty sharply about her food. *Why do you lie to me?* ect.

About 12:30 asked all hands to work against pain. Went for a drive taking Laura Sargent with her. Came back in distress. Asked all hands to work. Condition continued to become worse.

Sent for Wm. Bertram. East Boston - Old student. One of the deserters at the Chicago meeting. He came and did the work. Then we all worked all afternoon and evening.

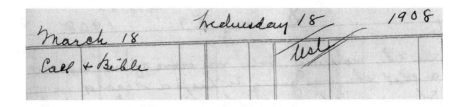

March 18   Wednesday 18   1908

Call & Bible

Letter to Kimball

Never rant over what should be killed & put out of sight. We can never kill a serpent or a tiger. They must have their day & kill themseves. Then they are dead. but nothing dies till it believes it is dead. Then it rots.

March.　　　　　Sunday 29　　　1908

Called in the morning. Told me none of us kept our
watch & that she was going to keep a record in a
book - Showed us the book - Tomlinson 1st ---. Clarks 2d
Dickey 3d all marked no

You must not let the mesmerism of mortal mind
make you think you can't keep your watch.

Opened the Bible at Matt 24-43. But know this
that if the good man of the house had known in what
watch the thief would come, he would have watched
If we are faithful over a few things we shall be made
ruler over many.

Do you understand this Mr Dickey? "Yes Mother"
Mr Tomlinson Yes Mother. Sarah Clark? Yes Mother.
Speak up I cannot hear you - yes mother.
Why don't you speak up so I can hear you?
Now Sarah Clark you are a big fat woman. Speak out.
--- so I can hear what you say.
(No louder) Yes Mother. Mrs Eddy mocking. yes mother. a ---

Anna Machacek whom Mrs Eddy requested me to
treat left for her home today - almost entirely well.
after Lathrop & Strang had each treated her two weeks.
I worked for her 10 days & she only had a slight trace
of rheumatism in her feet

Mrs Catt sent away on account of nervous belilfs. had been
under treatment. two weeks ago told Mrs McKenzie she
was all right.

March   Sunday 29   1908

Called us in the morning–Told me some of us kept our watch &
that she was going to keep a record in a book. Showed us the book
–Tomlinson 1st–Clark 2nd–Dickey 3rd–all marked no.
You must not let the mesmerism of mortal mind let you think you cannot keep your watch.
Opened the Bible at Matt 24-43. *But know this that if the good
man of the house had known at what watch the thief would come, he
would have watched. If we are faithful over a few things we shall be
made ruler over many.*
Do you understand this, Mr. Dickey? "Yes Mother." *Mr. Tomlinson?*
Yes, Mother. *Sarah Clark?* Yes, Mother. *Speak up, I can't hear you*–Yes,
Mother.
Why don't you speak up so I can hear you?
*Now Sarah Clark you are a big fat woman. Speak out - - -so I can
hear what you say.*
(No louder) Yes, Mother. Mrs. Eddy mocking *yes motherrrr,*
Anna Machacek** whom Mrs. Eddy requested me to treat left for
her home today—almost entirely well after Lathrop & Strang had
each treated her two weeks. I worked for her for 10 days & she had
only a slight trace of rheumatism in her feet.

Mrs. Cate sent away on acount of nervous beliefs, had been under
treatment two weeks ago talk Mrs. McKenzie she was all right.

**Anna Machacek is mentioned in the biography section of this
book as a devoted student who devoted her life to serving Mrs.

March   Monday 30   1908

Match * 1 no. * 2 yes * 3 no
new S + H. seals adopted today
Called 7 p.m. Now I want to say to you all that the
season of storms is coming on. The enemy - mesmerists -
claim they can do what they want with the weather,
just as they claim they can do as they will with
sickness. Now you all know you can control a headache or
a belief of dyspepsia + you are not afraid of it.
Sickness is a belief of mortal mind. Now what is a storm?
Is it not a false claim of material law? Is there any such
thing as material law? Then if bad weather or lightening
is an erroneous concept of mortal law - can't you break it up?
Now I want you to prepare yourselves to do this. I remember
once when we were having a terrific storm in belief + the
lightening was around the house like chains. The students
were with me + I declared to them that there was no
surplus electricity, + in a few minutes the whole storm
had disappeared.
Now you know there are no thunder storms in Divine Mind
- no lightening in heaven, so prepare yourselves to break up
these violent storms - There is no need for them.

This morning she said I shall not open the Bible for
you this morning, but upon being urged she consented +
opened at Scripture Proper names.
Then she closed it + said - There I no and no it is.

March   Monday 30   1908

Watch * 1 no *2 yes * 3 no
New S&H seals adopted today.
Called 7 p.m. *Now I want to say to you all that the season of storms is coming on. The enemy - mesmerists - claim they can do what they want with the weather just as they claim they can do as they will with sickness. Now you all know you can control a headache or a belief of dyspeptia* [sic] *and you are not afraid of it.*

Sickness is a belief of mortal mind. Now what is a storm? Is it not a false claim of material law? Is there any such thing as material law? Then if bad weather or lightening is an erroneous concept of mortal law can't you break it up? Now I want you to prepare yourselves to do this. I remember once when we were having a terrific storm in belief & the lightening was all around the house like chains. The students were with me & I declared to them that there was no surplus electricity, & in a few minutes the whole storm had disappeared.

Now you know there are no thunder storms in Divine Mind —no lightening in heaven, so prepare yourselves to break up these violent storms — There is no need for them.

This morning she said *I shall not open the Bible for you this morning* but upon being urged she consented & opened the Scripture. Proper names.

Then she closed it & said. *There I* [said] *no and no it is.*

April   Saturday 4   1908

All called 9.30 except Clark

*Now Mr. D if you had made your way over a road that was winding
& treacherous & you lost your way & found it again, wouldn't you profit
by the experience.*

Yes Mother.

*You will only learn to avoid the pitfalls by what you suffer, won't
you?*

Yes.

*Well, we learn that these pitfalls are no part of the road. So now we are
journeying along and we profit by what we suffer. "For whom the Lord
loveth he chastenth & scourgeth every son whom he receiveth." Heb 12.
"For our light affliction which is but for a moment worketh for us a far
more exceeding weight of glory" while we look not at the things which are
seen for the things which are seen are temporal: but the things which are
not seen are eternal. II Cor 4 17:18.*

April   Sunday 5   1908

All called 8-10 a.m. - walked over and sat down.

Who is the one who said, "I go in & went not." Matt 21: 3. Pointing
to me she said, *Thou art the man.* (with a laugh). I told her I thought
& felt my watch had been kept. Then she recited how she had passed
the night & it proved I had kept my watch.

Sarah Clark said she had strived to keep hers. Leader said *Strive to
enter in for straight* [sic] *is the gate & narrow is the way & few there be
who find it. Why did not the son go who said, "I go in."* Tomlinson said
"mesmerism." She said *yes but all sin is mesmerism* - I said because he
was satisfied with himself - *well that's nearer it but not quite.*

*It was because he had not repented. First we must see the error, then
repent & then forsake it. You will have to contend with sin until you have
overcome it. Then you will have another form of evil to meet - the envy &
jealousy of mortal mind because of your purity. That is where your Leader
stands.*

Dickey with a tame squirrel named Spike.

April   Monday 6   1908

All called 8:30 *I shall call you no more until you have risen higher — dismissed.*

I returned by myself in a few minutes and showed her where I had been reading II Cor 4:8-9. "We are troubled on every side yet not distressed, we are perplexed but not in despair: persecuted but not forsaken: cast down, but not destroyed."

I talked encouragingly to her & told her we could down this lie of discouragement - she seemed to brighten up & asked for my Bible which I had in my hand - She opened at the 34th chap of Ezekiel & read to the 15th verse. It seemed to impress her seriously & she seemed to apply it to herself.

After she called us all & seemed to be in a better mood & said *"I have called you because you have risen higher.* Things looked better for the day.

John Lathrop arrived at 4 p.m.

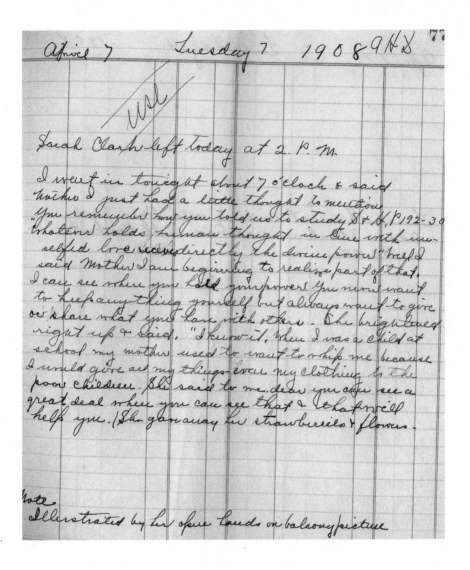

April 7   Tuesday 7   1908

Sarah Clark left today at 2 pm.

I went in tonight at about 7 o'clock and said, "Mother I just had a little thought to mention. You remember how you told us to study S&H P 192: 30. "Whatever holds thought in line with unselfed love receives directly the divine power" well I said Mother I am beginning to realize part of that. I can see where you hold your power. You never want to keep anything yourself but always want to give or share what you have with others. She brightened right up & said, *I know it. When I was a child at school my mother used to want to whip me because I would give all my things even my clothing to the poor children. She said to me dear you can see a great deal when you can see that & that will help you.* (She gave away her strawberries & flowers.[)]

Note
    Illustrated by her open hands on balcony picture.

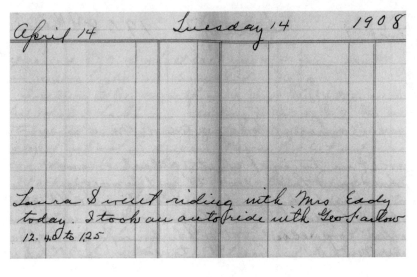

April 14   Tuesday 14   1908

Laura S. went riding with Mrs. Eddy today. I took an auto ride with Geo Farlow 12.40 to 1.25

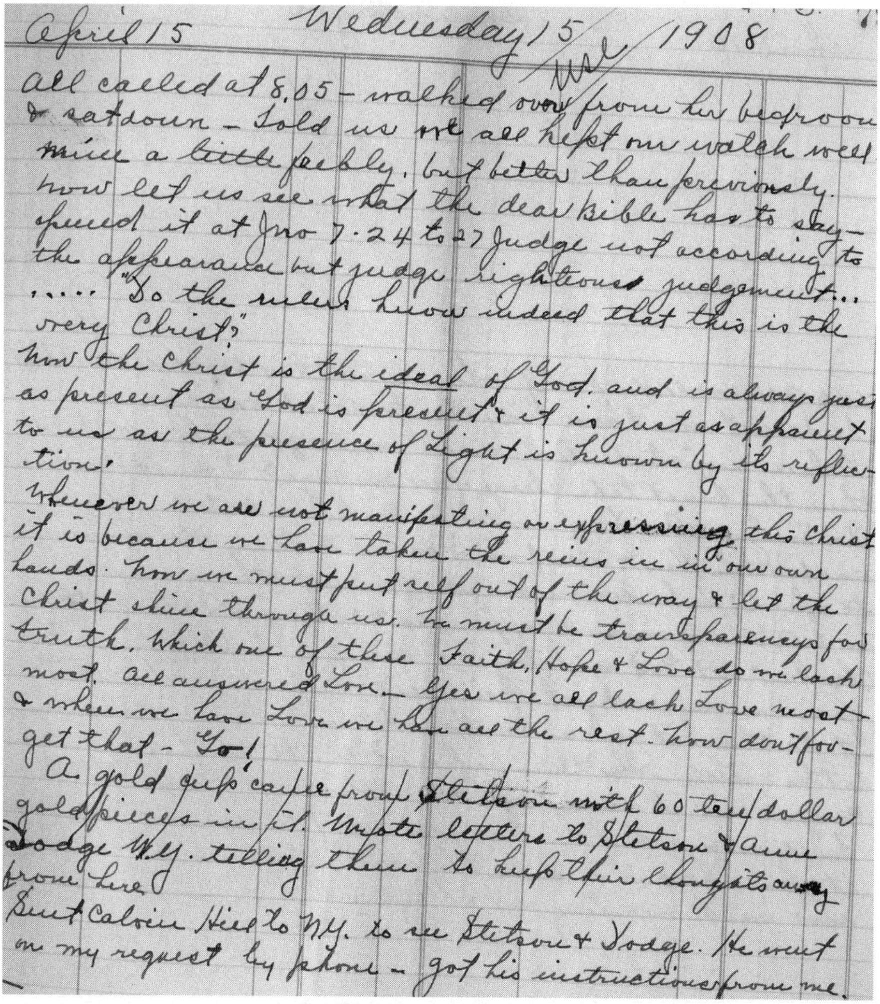

[Handwritten journal entry reproduced in print below]

April 15   Wednesday 15   1908

All called at 8:05 - walked over from her bedroom and sat down -Told us we all kept our watch well, voice a little feebly, but better than previously.

Now let us see what the dear Bible has to say—opened it at Jno 7-24 to 27 *Judge not according the appearance but judge righteous judgement....* "*Do the rulers know that this is the very Christ?*"

Now the Christ is the <u>ideal</u> of God, and is always just as present as God is present & it is just as apparent to us as the presence of Light is known by its reflection.

Whenever we are not manifesting or expressing this Christ it is because we have taken the reins in our own hands. Now we must put self out of the way & let the Christ shine through us. We must be transparencys [*sic*] *for truth. Which one of these Faith, Hope and Love do we lack most. All* answered Love–*Yes we all lack Love most & when we have Love we have all the rest. Now don't forget that–Go!*

A gold cup came from Stetson with 60 ten-dollar gold pieces in it.

Wrote letters to Stetson & Annie Dodge. N.Y. telling them to keep their thoughts away from here.

Sent Calvin Hill to N.Y. to see Stetson & Dodge. He went on my request by phone–got his instructions from me.

Calvin Hill beg
an assisting Mrs Eddy in 1899, and after her passing, he became superintendent of the Mother Church Sunday school and served on the Finance Committee. His account, and others of Mrs. Eddy's close followers, are available for research at the Mary Baker Eddy Library.

It is important when one is trying to understand the full picture of life in the Chestnut Hill family that at least these several sources be considered: Laura Sargent, Irving Tomlinson, Calvin Frye and William Rathvon all wrote accounts. Hill states, for instance, in his reminiscences that when Ira Knapp died, Mrs. Eddy offered his board position to Calvin Frye, but he declined; then Dickey lobbied for the position and got it.

Homeward Part II: Chestnut Hill by Steven R. Howard from the Longyear Museum has valuable information on this period.

80
April 16 Thursday 16 1908 AHB

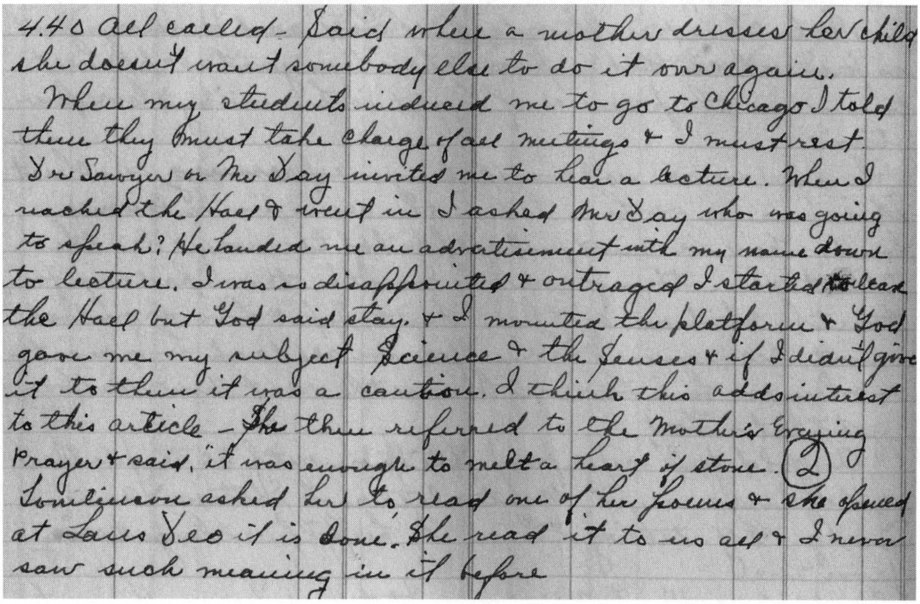

4.40 All called - Said when a mother dresses her child
she doesn't want somebody else to do it over again.
When my students induced me to go to Chicago I told
them they must take charge of all meetings & I must rest.
Dr Sawyer or Mr Day invited me to hear a lecture. When I
reached the Hall & went in I asked Mr Day who was going
to speak? He handed me an advertisement with my name down
to lecture. I was so disappointed & outraged I started to leave
the Hall but God said stay. & I mounted the platform & God
gave me my subject Science & the Senses & if I didn't give
it to them it was a caution. I think this adds interest
to this article - She then referred to the Mother's Evening
Prayer & said, it was enough to melt a heart of stone. (2)
Tomlinson asked her to read one of her poems & she opened
at Laus Deo it is done. She read it to us all & I never
saw such meaning in it before

April 16 Thursday 16 1908

4:40 All called–Said *when a mother dresses her child she doesn't want somebody else to do it over again.*

When my students induced me to go to Chicago I told them they must take charge of all meetings & I must rest. Dr. Sawyer or Mr. Day invited me to hear a lecture. When I reached the Hall & went in I asked Mr. Day who was going to speak? He handed me an advertisement with my name down to lecture. I was so disappointed & outraged I started to leave the Hall but God said stay, & I mounted the platform & God gave me my subject Science & the Senses & if I didn't give to them it was a caution. I think this adds interest to this article –

She then referred to the Mother's Evening Prayer & said, it was enough to melt a heart of stone.

Tomlinson asked her to read one of her poems & she opened at Laus Deo it is done. She read it to us all & I never saw such meaning in it before.

Dickey's room also contained a large Wooten desk on which rested a typewriter. Typewriting had become a useful skill during the 1890s and Dickey made good use of it for letters. He seems to have taken his small Kodak and, with someone's assistance, photographed his room from every vantage point.

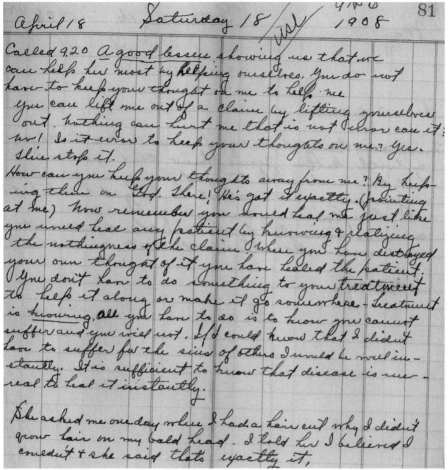

April 18   Saturday 18   1908

Called 9.20 <u>A</u> <u>good</u> <u>lesson</u> showing us that we can help her most by helping ourselves. *You do not have to keep your thought on me to help me. You can lift me out of a claim by lifting yourselves out. Nothing can hurt me that is not error, can it? no! Is it error to keep your thoughts on me? Yes. Then stop it.*

How can you keep your thoughts away from me? By keeping them on God. *There! He's got it exactly.* (pointing at me*) Now remember you could heal me just like you could heal any patient by knowing & realizing the nothingness of the claim. When you have destroyed your own thought of it you have healed the patient. You don't have to do something to your treatment to help it along or make it go somewhere–Treatment is <u>knowing</u>. All you have to do is to know you cannot suffer and you will not. If I could know that I did not have to suffer for the sins of others I would* *be well instantly. It is sufficient to know that disease is unreal to heal it instantly.*

She asked me one day when I had a hair cut why I didn't grow hair on my bald head. I told her I believed I couldn't & she said that's exactly it.

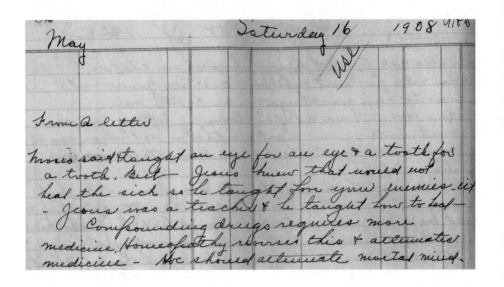

May   Saturday 16   1908

From a letter

Moses said & taught an eye for an eye & a tooth for a tooth But – Jesus knew that would not heal the sick so he taught Love your enemies ect. Jesus was a teacher and he taught how to heal –

Compounding drugs requires more medicine, Homeopathy reverses this & attenuates medicine. We should attenuate mortal mind.

An elm that could have been a favorite of Mrs. Eddy was presumably photographed by Dickey. On the back of the photo he wrote "The Mary Baker Eddy elm." Not much more is known about it than that. Mrs. Eddy did mention in Miscellaneous Writings *that she had admired the elm tree on the Congregational Church grounds in Concord.*

May   Sunday 17   1908

All called 2 P.M. on what seemed to be a continuation of last Sunday's talk. *Now can't you all get out of addition? You do not have to stay in addition all the time. If you have the same Principle it is just as easy (& in fact easier) to multiply than it is to add. You must rise out of the addition of C.S. and let God – Divine Mind multiply through you.*

All called at 5.45 & given a long talk about letting material things hinder our progress in Science. It is a trick of the devil to keep us chasing after matter - You cannot serve God & Mammon.

I was called alone at 8 pm. It was dark in her room and when I went in she said, *Can you see me?* I said Yes Mother. She said *I can see you by the light of your countenance.* Then she said she just called me to say that my answers before supper had pleased her so much. *Adam Dickey you are not the old Adam you are the new Adam & I want you to be a good healer. When you are a good healer you are all you can be. Do you understand that?* I said Yes Mother. When I get close enough to God to heal quickly I will have all else. She said *that's just exactly it. Good night dear—*

The parlor at Chestnut Hill.

Hoag   Lathrop   Wilcox
May   Thursday 21   1908

All called 8.20. Showing the difference between spiritual understanding & Material sense. We cannot have good God and Good devil. What is a good dinner or a good meal, good devil. What is a good night's sleep – good evil. What is a nice new dress – good evil. What is a sense of health in matter – good evil – which is nearer God a human sense of health or a sense of sickness? A sense of sickness. What is it then that brings us into a

*realization of true being – Spiritual understanding. Then how do I (*Mrs.
E*) heal – by knowing that the Omnipotent Everpresent Eternal & Infinite Mind is All & therefore there is no inaction diseased action – reaction
– or over action.*
Spiritual understanding – a knowledge of God makes perfect.

John Lathrop arrived this a.m. to take Mrs. Hoag's place but that
old belief had not been met & he was sent back to New York at once
– stayed for dinner.

Mrs. Wilcox elevated from housekeeper to worker & moved into
the yellow room.

divine law – that error cannot injure us when we are asleep. This
is <u>important</u> for the enemy is at work on this & we must head them
off.

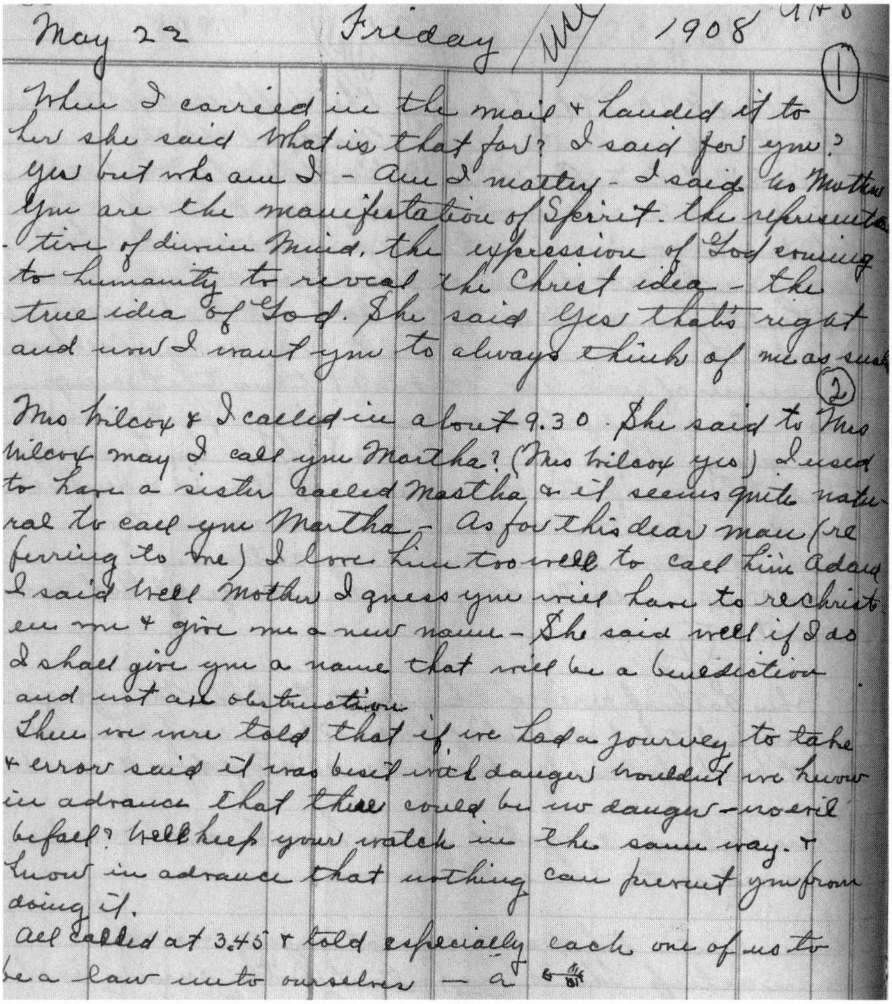
May 22 Friday 1908
(1)
When I carried in the mail + handed it to her she said What is that for? I said for you? Yes but who am I - Am I matter - I said No Mother You are the manifestation of Spirit the representa-tive of divine Mind, the expression of God coming to humanity to reveal the Christ idea - the true idea of God. She said Yes that's right and now I want you to always think of me as such
(2)
Mrs Wilcox & I called in about 9.30. She said to Mrs Wilcox may I call you Martha? (Mrs Wilcox yes) I used to have a sister called Martha & it seems quite natural to call you Martha - As for this dear man (referring to me) I love him too well to call him Adam. I said Well Mother I guess you will have to rechristen me + give me a new name - She said well if I do I shall give you a name that will be a benediction and not an obstruction
Then we were told that if we had a journey to take + error said it was beset with danger wouldn't we know in advance that there could be no danger - no evil befall? Well keep your watch in the same way + know in advance that nothing can prevent you from doing it.
All called at 3.45 + told especially each one of us to be a law unto ourselves — a

May 22 Friday 1908

When I carried in the mail and handed it to her she said *What is that for*? I said for you? *Yes but who am I - am I matter* - I said No Mother. You are the manifestation of Spirit the representative of divine Mind, the expression of God coming to humanity to reveal the Christ idea - the true idea of God. She said *Yes that's right and now I want you to always think of me as such.*

Mrs. Wilcox & I called in about 9.30. She said to Mrs. Wilcox *may I call you Martha* (Mrs. Wilcox yes) *I used to have a sister called Martha & it seems quite natural to call you Martha - As for this dear man* (referring to me) *I love him too well to call him Adam.* I said well Mother I guess you will have to rechristen me & give me a new name - She said *well if I do I shall give you a name that will be a benediction and not an obstruction* [S&H p. 338].

Then we were told that if we had a journey to take & error said it was beset with danger wouldn't we know in advance that there could be no danger - no evil befall? *Well, keep your watch in this same way & know in advance that nothing can prevent you from doing it.*

All called at 3.45 & told especially each one of us to be a law unto ourselves—

Dickey' retained this photo of Pleasant View which might have been taken by someone else much earlier; the vines are not fully grown. As a board member Dickey later supervised the tearing down of the house when it grew dilapidated.

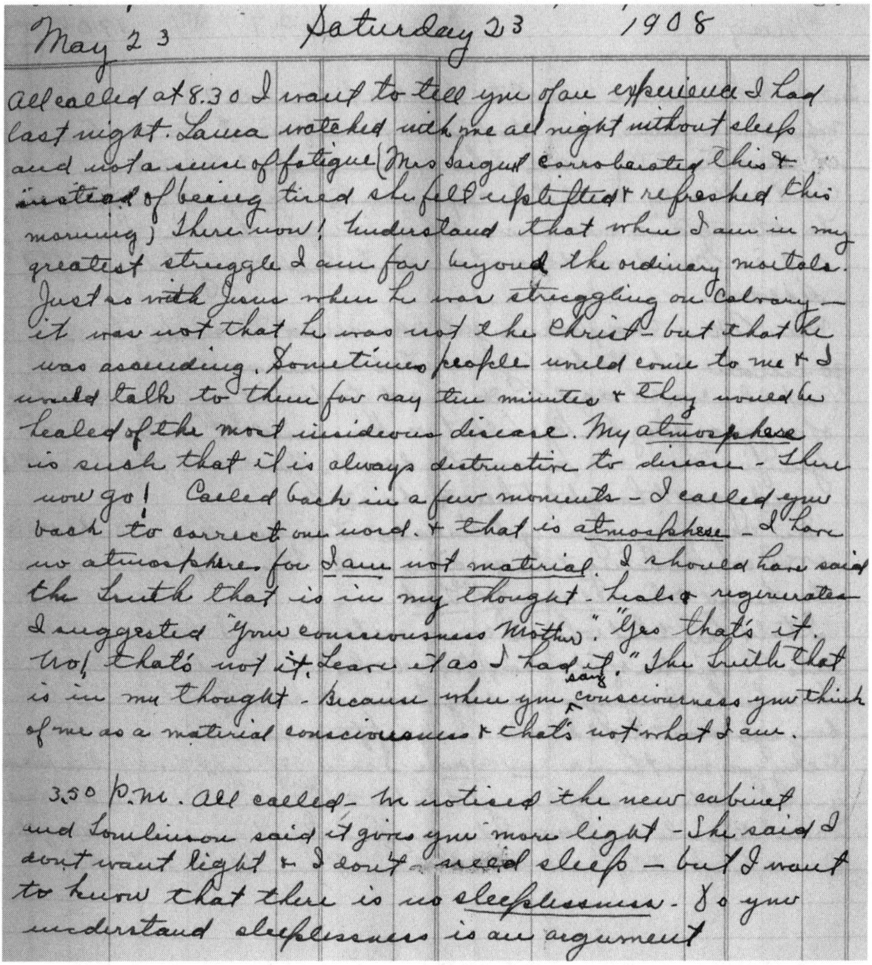

[Handwritten journal entry, reproduced below in typeset form:]

May 23   Saturday 23   1908

All called at 8.30 I want to tell you of an experience I had last night. Laura watched with me all night without sleep and not a sense of fatigue (Mrs Sargent corroborating this & instead of being tired she felt uplifted & refreshed this morning) There now! Understand that when I am in my greatest struggle I am far beyond the ordinary mortals. Just so with Jesus when he was struggling on Calvary — it was not that he was not the Christ — but that he was ascending. Sometimes people would come to me & I would talk to them for say ten minutes & they would be healed of the most insidious disease. My atmosphere is such that it is always destructive to disease — There now go! Called back in a few moments — I called you back to correct one word. & that is atmosphere — I have no atmosphere for I am not material. I should have said the truth that is in my thought — heals & regenerates I suggested "your consciousness Mother." "Yes that's it. No, that's not it. Leave it as I had said." The truth that is in my thought — because when you consciousness you think of me as a material consciousness & that's not what I am.

3.30 p.m. All called — We noticed the new cabinet and Tomlinson said it gives you more light — She said I dont want light & I dont need sleep — but I want to know that there is no sleeplessness — So you understand sleeplessness is an argument

May 23   Saturday 23   1908

All called at 8:30. *I want to tell you of an experience I had last night. Laura watched with me all night without sleep and not a sense of fatigue.* (Mrs. Sargent corroborated this & instead of being tired she felt uplifted & refreshed this morning) *There now! Understand that when I am in my greatest struggle I am far beyond the ordinary mortals. Just as with Jesus where he was struggling on Calvary - it was not that he was not the Christ - but that he was ascending. Sometimes people would come* *to me & I would talk to them for say ten minutes & they would be healed of the most insidious disease. My <u>atmosphere</u> is such that it is always destructive to disease – There now go!* Called back in a few moments – *I called you back to correct one word and that is atmosphere. I have no atmosphere for <u>I am not material</u>. I should have said the Truth that is in my thought heals & regenerates.* I suggested "Your consciousness Mother." *Yes, that's it. No, that's not it. Leave it as I had it. The Truth that is in my thought – Because when you say consciousness you think of me as a material consciousness and that's not what I am.*

3.50 p.m. All called – we noticed the new cabinet and Tomlinson said it gives you more light – She said I don't want light & I don't need sleep – but I want to know that there is no <u>sleeplessness</u>. Do you understand sleeplessness is an argument.

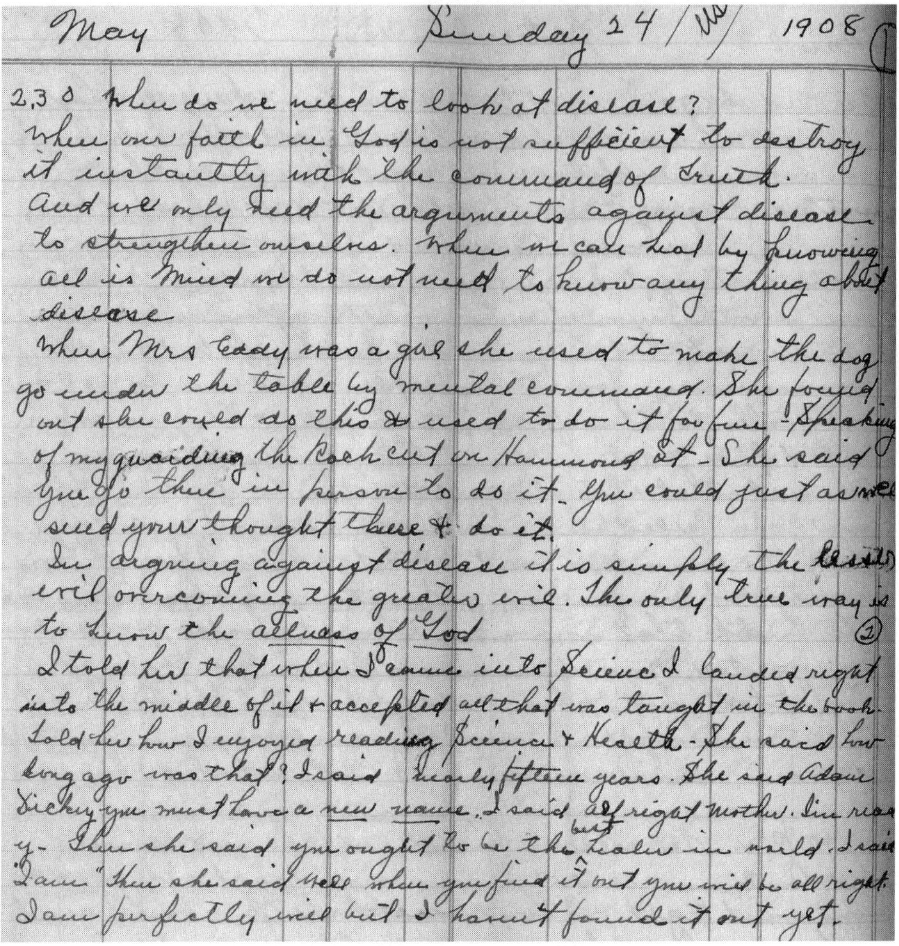
May Sunday 24 / [illegible] / 1908

2.30 When do we need to look at disease?
When our faith in God is not sufficient to destroy
it instantly with the command of Truth.
And we only need the arguments against disease
to strengthen ourselves. When we can heal by knowing
all is Mind we do not need to know any thing about
disease
When Mrs Eddy was a girl she used to make the dog
go under the table by mental command. She found
out she could do this & used to do it for fun - Speaking
of my guarding the Rock cut on Hammond St - She said
You go there in person to do it. You could just as well
send your thought there & do it.
In arguing against disease it is simply the lesser
evil overcoming the greater evil. The only true way is
to know the allness of God (2)
I told her that when I came into Science I landed right
into the middle of it & accepted all that was taught in the book.
told her how I enjoyed reading Science & Health - She said how
long ago was that? I said nearly fifteen years. She said Adam
Dickey you must have a new name. I said all right mother. Im rea
y- Then she said you ought to be the best healer in world. I said
"I am" Then she said well when you find it out you will be all right.
I am perfectly well but I haven't found it out yet.

May Sunday 24 1908

2.30 *When do we need to look at disease? When our faith in God is not sufficient to destroy it instantly with the command of Truth. And we only need the arguments against disease to strengthen ourselves. When we can heal by knowing all is Mind we do not need to know anything about disease.*

When Mrs. Eddy was a girl she used to make the dog go under the table by mental command. She found out she could do this & used to do it for fun. Speaking of my guarding the Rock cut on Hammond St–She said You go there in person to do it. You could just as well send your thought there and do it.

In arguing against disease it is simply the lesser evil overcoming the greater evil. The only true way is to know the <u>allness</u> <u>of</u> <u>God</u>.

I told her that when I came into Science I landed right into the middle of it & accepted all that was taught in the book. Told her how I enjoyed reading Science & Health. She said how long ago was that? I said nearly fifteen years. She said *Adam Dickey you must have a <u>new</u> <u>name</u>.* I said "all right Mother, I'm ready." Then she said *You ought to be the best healer in* [the] *world.* I said "I am." Then she said, *Well, when you find it out you will be all right. I am perfectly well but I haven't found it out yet.*

May 25   Monday 25   1908

8 PM. I went in alone & said as she extended her two hands to me. I have just come in to tell you how much I love you - *well* she said *I never could tell you how much I love you.*

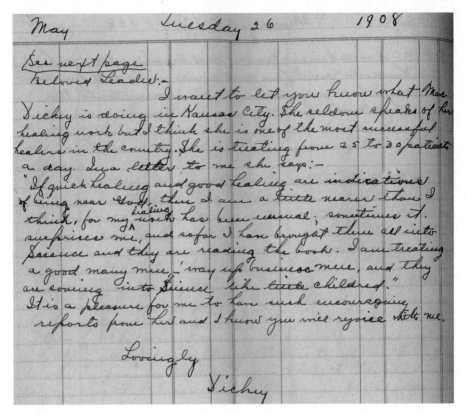

May   Tuesday 26   1908

<u>See next page</u>

Beloved Leader:–

I want to let you know what Mrs. Dickey is doing in Kansas City. She seldom speaks of her healing work but I think she is one of the most successful healers in the country. She is treating from 25 to 30 patients a day. In a letter to me she says:–

"If quick healing and good healing are indications of being near God, then I am a little nearer than I think, for my healing work has been unusual; sometimes it surprises me, and so far I have brought them all into Science and they are reading the book. I am treating a good many more 'way up' business men, and they are coming into Science like little children."

It is a pleasure for me to have such encouraging reports from her and I know you will rejoice with me.

Lovingly
Dickey

Lillian Dickey was an active practitioner and teacher in Kansas City, Missouri.

May 27   Wednesday 27   1908

I took the foregoing note to her after reading it.
She said yes I should think you would rejoice and now
let me tell you something: but you must never tell it
to any one not even to your wife until you think she is
ready for it & God will tell you when. It is this – When
a student puts my book in the hands of a patient and
knows that he will receive it – the work is done. I said
Yes Mother I believe it. She said – but let me tell you
dear don't tell it to a student. – don't let any one know
it – for that is what is causing my struggle
I said Mother do you mean that you suffer while they
read your book and are healed? She started up in her
chair & seizing both my hands she said. "I'll not say it because
it is a lie" I said I understand you Mother & I'll keep you
to meet that & know that it is a lie. She said So darling
– do know it for me & keep me to know it.

     Then she looked at me in the tenderest way & said –
when I give you a present (She made a present to the
coachman & overseer of an emerald pin set in 8 small
diamonds – through me this afternoon) I think I
shall have to take it from here (placing her hand over
her heart) I said Mother, that's the only present I want.
When I have that I can never lose it. She smiled assent
& I left the room.

     Took Hayne Davis letter telling her he would ——

         tone page here all rest missing

May 27 Wednesday 27 1908

I took the foregoing note to her after reading it. She said Y*es, I should think you would rejoice and now let me tell you something; but you must never tell it to anyone not even to your wife until you think she is ready for it & God will tell you when. It is this - when a student puts my book in the hands of a patient and knows that he will receive it - the work is done.* I said Yes Mother I believe it. But she said - *but let me tell you dear - don't tell it to a student - don't let anyone know it - for that is causing my struggle.* I said Mother do you mean that you suffer while they read your book and are healed? She started up in her chair and seizing both my hands she said, *I'll not say it because it is a lie.* I said I understand you Mother & I'll help you to meet that & know that it is a lie." She said *So darling - do know it for me and help me to know it.*

Then she looked up at me in the tenderest way and said - *When I give you a present* (She made a present to the coachman & overseer of an emerald pin set in 8 small diamonds - through me this afternoon) *I think I shall have to take it from here* (placing her hand over her heart) I said Mother, that's the only present I want. When I have that I can never lose it. She smiled assent & I left the room.

Took Hayne Davis' letter telling him he would——

Torn page here—all rest missing

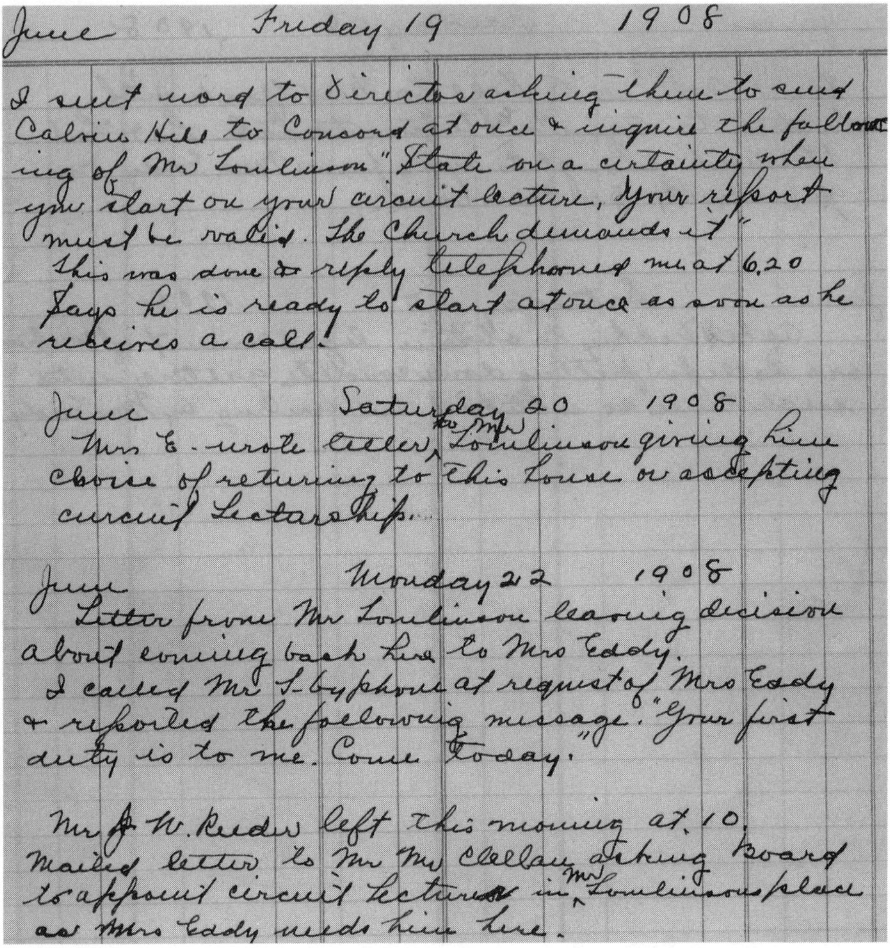
June Friday 19 1908
I sent word to Directors asking them to send
Calvin Hill to Concord at once & inquire the follow-
ing of Mr Tomlinson "State on a certainty when
you start on your circuit lecture, Your report
must be valid. The Church demands it"
This was done & reply telephoned me at 6.20
Says he is ready to start at once as soon as he
receives a call.

June Saturday 20 1908
Mrs E. wrote letter to Mr Tomlinson giving him
choice of returning to this house or accepting
circuit Lectureship...

June Monday 22 1908
Letter from Mr Tomlinson leaving decision
about coming back here to Mrs Eddy.
I called Mr T. by phone at request of Mrs Eddy
& reported the following message. "Your first
duty is to me. Come today."

Mr J. W. Reeder left this morning at 10.
Mailed letter to Mr McClellan asking board
to appoint circuit lecturer in Mr Tomlinson's place
as Mrs Eddy needs him here.

June Friday 19 1908

I sent word to Directors asking them to send Calvin Hill to Concord at once & inquire the following of Mr. Tomlinson. "State on a certainty when you start on your circuit lecture. Your report must be valid. The Church demands it."

This was done & reply telephoned me at 6.20. Says he is ready to start at once as soon as he receives a call.

June Saturday 20 1908

Mrs. E wrote letter to Mr. Tomlinson giving him choice of returning to this house or accepting circuit Lectureship.

June   Monday 22   1908
Letter from Mr. Tomlinson leaving decision about coming back
here to Mrs. Eddy.

I called Mr. T by phone at request of Mrs. Eddy & reported the
following message. *Your first duty is to me. Come today.*

Mr. J.W. Reeder left this morning at 10. Mailed letter to Mr. Mc-
Clellan asking Board to appoint circuit Lecturer in Mr. Tomlinson's
place as Mrs. Eddy needs him here.

Harpwell, Maine, often drew Adam Dickey and his family
for summer jaunts. It isn't likely that he spent time there while
he was with Mrs. Eddy; she did not believe in vacations. This
postcard view he kept was color-tinted.

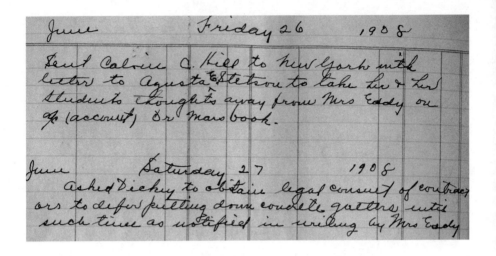

June   Friday 26   1908
Sent Calvin C. Hill to New York with letter to A[u]gusta E. Stetson to take her & her students thoughts away from Mrs. Eddy on (account) Dr. Mars book.*

June   Saturday 27   1908
Asked Dickey to obtain legal consult of contractors to defer putting down concrete gutters until such time as notified in writing by Mrs. Eddy.

---

* Gerhardt C. Mars, *The Interpretation of Life In Which is Shown the Relation of Modern Culture to Christian Science* published in New York in 1908. The book gives an interesting analysis of the history of human thought, which culminated in Mrs. Eddy's discovering of Christian Science. Mrs. Eddy quickly wrote a commentary of the book, saying she had neither read nor endorsed the book, despite claims to the contrary. She added, "Christian Scientists are not concerned with philosophy; divine Science is all they need, or can have in reality."

Courtesy Mary Baker Eddy Collection.

William Rathvon was at Chestnut Hill during the same years as Dickey. He was not one of Dickey's strongest supporters both during the years in the home and later on the Board of The First Church of Christ, Scientist, Boston.

July   Sunday 5   Science & Health

All called 8.30 - Told Wilcox she didn't heed her watch & also
said if she didn't keep it she would put her back as maid.
(But Wilcox said she wouldn't go back) Told us how
she apparently contradicted herself sometimes, but she always
obeys the voice of God.
It comes to me and I say it when I wrote S & H. ①
I felt like a machine & simply wrote what came to me.
& every day after the sun went down every thing would
stop & I would have nothing to say & next day I would
wait until the thoughts came before I would write.
Now I am like the rest of you, trying to work up to
what is in that book. Sometimes I am astonished at
what I find there & see that I cannot attained 1 millioneth
of what the book calls for. It is a wonderful book & covers
eternity. Now that's my confidence in God, - My confidence
in myself is that I have directed this movement for forty
years & it is still thriving always, waiting for God's directions
- always receiving them. My books contain no contradictions when they are understood. The By-laws calling
for the appointment of a circuit Lecturer I have held up
for a while for a certain purpose & am now waiting to
see whether we shall have a nature of England, B.
or the U.S.

July   Sunday 5   1908   Science & Health

All called 8:30. Told Wilcox she didn't keep her watch & also said if she didn't keep it she would put her back as maid. (But Wilcox said she wouldn't go back.) Told us how she apparently contradicted herself sometimes, but she always obeys the voice of God.

It comes to me and I say it. When I wrote S&H I felt like a machine & simply wrote what came to me & every day after the sun went down everything would stop & I would have nothing to say & next day I would wait until the thoughts came before I would write. Now I am like the rest of you, trying to work up to what is in that book. Sometimes I am astonished at what I find there & see that I haven't attained 1 millionth of what the book calls for. It is a wonderful book & covers eternity. Now that's my confidence in God. My confidence in myself is that I have directed this movement for forty years & it is still thriving always waiting for God's directions - always receiving them. My books contain no contradictions when they are understood. The By-laws calling for the appointment of a circuit Lecturer I have held up for a while for a certain purpose & am now waiting to see whether we shall have a native of England or the U.S.

Coming and going and serving at Chestnut Hill

Martha W. Wilcox, C.S. B., who had been a school teacher in Kansas City, was in Mrs. Eddy's household for two and a half years. She had primary class instruction in 1903 and became a student in Bicknell Young's 1910 Normal Class. For thirty-six years she served the cause of Christian Science.

Irving Tomlinson, C.S.B., was a member of Mrs. Eddy's last class and was one of the first of five lecturers. He was part of the household from time to time 1908-1910. He lectured until 1935, then devoted his full time to the practice and teaching of Christian Science.

Judge Clifford P. Smith, C.S. B., became a leading advocate for the rights of Christian Scientists to heal through prayer. He conducted Mrs. Eddy's funeral services and served the church in many leadership capacities from 1910 through the 20s and 30s.

James A. Neal, C.S.D., studied with Mrs. Eddy in her March Primary Class of 1889 and her last class in 1898. He served his leader in many capacities and after her passing as a member of the board of The Mother Church and as trustee of the Benevolent Association.

John Lathrop, C. S. B., had been at Pleasant View with Mrs. Eddy, sometimes serving as her secretary, and went on to serve during the Chestnut Hill years in many other capacities for the movement. He was the son of Laura Lathrop.

Ella W. Hoag, C.S.D., had class instruction with Mrs. Eddy in 1888. She served Mrs. Eddy at Chestnut Hill from 1908-1910. She was later the first woman president of The Mother Church.

Sarah J. Clark, C.S.D., had edited *The Christian Science Journal*. She served at Chestnut Hill in 1908.

Alfred Farlow, C.S.D., skilled in public relations, was the first manager of the Committee on Publication for the Mother Church. He was one of five members of the Farlow family to embrace Christian Science; his brother is mentioned as taking Dickey for an automobile ride.

Information on early pioneers in Christian Science is found in the Longyear Foundation's *Pioneers in Christian Science* and also in the series *We Knew Mary Baker Eddy.*

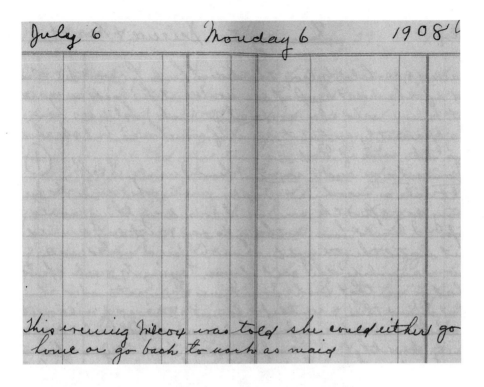

July 6   Monday 6   1908

This evening Wilcox was told she could either go home or go back to work as maid.

The construction of the Extension to the Mother Church was a major step in the growth of the movement and required the personal attention of Mrs. Eddy. Later, after Dickey arrived and in the years 1908–1910, she left its management to the Board of Directors. Dickey kept a series of photos of the construction of the Extension.

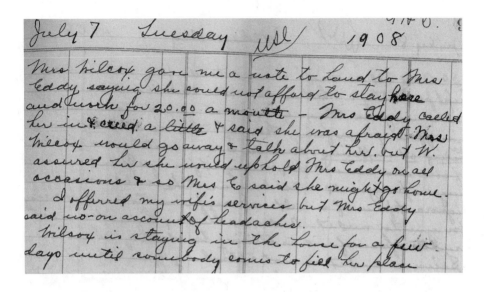

July 7   Tuesday   1908

Mrs. Wilcox gave me a note to hand to Mrs. Eddy saying she could not afford to stay here and work for 20.00 a month.- Mrs. Eddy called her in and cried a little & said she was afraid Mrs. Wilcox would go away & talk about her but W. assured her she would uphold Mrs. Eddy on all occasions & so Mrs.E said she might go home.

I offerred [sic] my wife's services but Mrs. Eddy said no - on account of headaches.

Wilcox is staying in the house for a few days until somebody comes to fill her place.

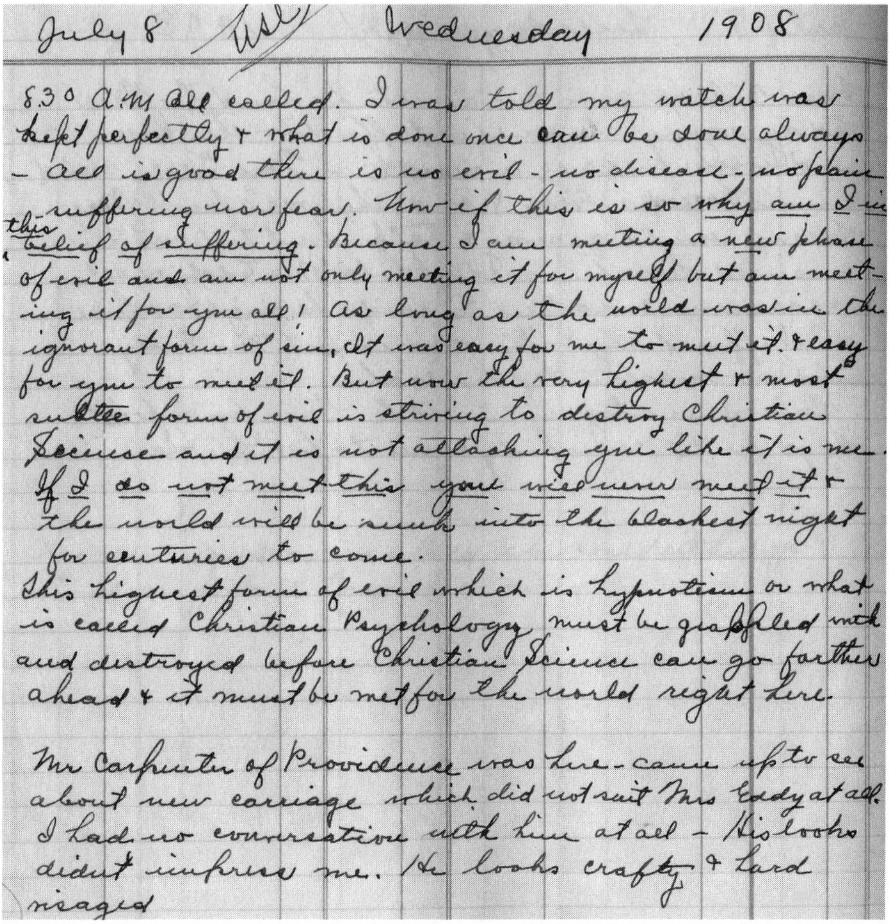
July 8 Wednesday 1908

8.30 a.m. All called. I was told my watch was kept perfectly & what is done once can be done always - all is good there is no evil - no disease - no pain suffering nor fear. Now if this is so why am I in this belief of suffering. Because I am meeting a new phase of evil and am not only meeting it for myself but am meeting it for you all! As long as the world was in the ignorant form of sin, it was easy for me to meet it. & easy for you to meet it. But now the very highest & most subtle form of evil is striving to destroy Christian Science and it is not attacking you like it is me. If I do not meet this you will never meet it & the world will be sunk into the blackest night for centuries to come.
This highest form of evil which is hypnotism or what is called Christian Psychology, must be grappled with and destroyed before Christian Science can go farther ahead & it must be met for the world right here.

Mr Carpenter of Providence was here - came up to see about new carriage which did not suit Mrs Eddy at all. I had no conversation with him at all - His looks didnt impress me. He looks crafty & hard visaged

July 8 Wednesday 1908

8:30 A.M. All called. I was told my watch was kept perfectly & *what is done once can be done always - all is good there is no evil - no disease - no pain suffering nor fear. Now if this is so <u>why</u> <u>am</u> <u>I</u> <u>in</u> <u>this</u> <u>belief</u> <u>of</u> <u>suffering</u>. Because I am meeting a <u>new</u> phase of evil and am not only meeting it for myself but am meeting it for you all! As long as the world was in the ignorant form of sin it was easy for me to meet it & easy for you to meet it. But now the very highest & most subtle form of evil is striving to destroy Christian Science and it is not attacking you like it is me. <u>If</u> <u>I</u> <u>do</u> <u>not</u> <u>meet</u> <u>this</u> <u>you</u> <u>will</u> <u>never</u> <u>meet</u> <u>it</u> & the world will be sunk into the blackest night for centuries to come.*
This highest form of evil which is hypnotism or what is called Christian Psychology, must be grappled with destroyed before Christian Science can

go farther ahead & it must be met for the world right here.

Mr. Carpenter of Providence was here – came up to see about new carriage which did not suit Mrs. Eddy at all. I had no conversations with him at all – His looks didn't impress me. He looks crafty & hard-visaged.

Gilbert C. Carpenter about 1905.

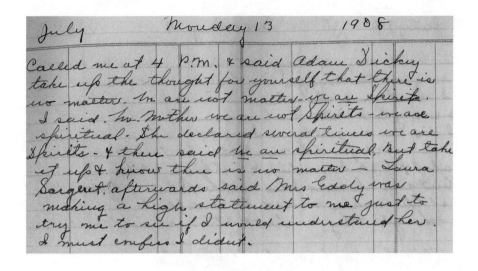

July   Monday 13   1908

Called me at 4 p.m. & said *Adam Dickey take up the thought for yourself that there is no matter. We are not matter - we are Spirits*. I said No, Mother we are not Spirits - we are spiritual. She declared several times *we are Spirits -* & then said *We are spiritual. But take it up & know there is no matter -* Laura Sargent afterwards said Mrs. Eddy was making a high statement to me just to try me to see if I would understand her. I must confess I didn't.

July 14   Tuesday 14   1908

A bad day all day: at about 11:45 she was lying on the lounge in her room & called for me. I went in & she asked me to take her in my arms & carry her into her bedroom & put her on the bed. I did so as gently as I could – she would not have me work for her mentally, but did call for me about 8:30. I went in & worked audibly for a while but she said I did not help her. In fact none of the workers seemed to be able to help her although they worked and strove almost constantly.

Mrs. Eddy did not drive out today.

July 28   Tuesday 28   1908

In a letter to the Board of Directors Mrs. Eddy said, *So soon as the Publishing house debt is paid I request the CS Board of Directors to start a daily newspaper called "Christian Science Monitor." This must be done without fail.* M.B.G.E.

This is the second time she spoke to me about starting a daily newspaper - once about a month ago or more. She told me to give orders to start this daily, but when I spoke to Frye about it he said we had enough trouble on our hands now without a daily newspaper & for me to drop the subject. I spoke to Mr. McLellan about it but he also talked against it, & as I had no definite instructions, I could do nothing although the idea struck me as a capital one & I strongly hoped it would go through.

00 September   Saturday 5   1908   A H 5
                                        (Mr. McClellan)

Mrs Eady gave me a beautiful amethyst ring today
This morning before breakfast Mrs Eddy called me into
her bedroom & said Mr Dickey could you serve as my
trustee - I said not as well as Mr McClellan. He has
been so faithful & so competent - She interrupted me & intimated I was being handled by mesmerism - & sent
me from the room. Outside I met Mrs Sargent - she
said Mr Dickey what did you say that for. When Mother
is determined to do any thing like this (meaning
to let Mr McClellan resign as trustee) don't you
go against her. Go back at once & tell her you see
your mistake & you will do any thing she wants -
I did so & she seemed so pleased & said "thank God
the mesmerism is broken" Then she said - "There dear
you have answered my question thank you" & I left.
To day afternoon - took a letter from Mrs Eddy to
Mr McClellan containing I don't know what & the reply
was that he had no desire for office & inclosing his resignation from three offices - Director in the Mother Church -
trustee of her estate - & Editor in chief of the C S Magazines. Frye gave the replies to me & I opened them & gave
them to Mrs Eddy. She dictated a reply accepting his resignation to all but Editor saying she wished him to retain
that for the present. I sent the letter to his house by
Mr Salchow & he got it on his return from Concord & he
called me up by phone acknowledging receipt of letter.
has been rainy all day.   Farlow still here.

September 5 continued Saturday 5   1908
On the afternoon Mrs Eddy asked me again if I would
serve as her trustee & I said Yes Mother I will
serve in any position where God puts me.

September   Saturday 5   1908 (Mr. McClellan)

Mrs. Eddy gave me a beautiful amethyst ring today. This morning before breakfast Mrs. Eddy called me into her bedroom & said *Mr. Dickey could you serve as my Trustee* - I said not as well as Mr. McClellan. He has been so faithful & so competent - She interrupted me & intimated I was being handled by mesmerism & sent me from the room. Outside I met Mrs. Sargent - she said Mr. Dickey what did you say that for - when Mother is determined to do any thing like this (meaning to let Mr. McClellan resign as trustee) don't you go against her. Go back at once & tell her you see your mistake & you will do anything she wants - I did so & she seemed so pleased & said *Thank God the mesmerism is broken.* Then she said, *There dear you have answered my question. Thank you.* & I left.

Today Stevenson took a letter from Mrs. Eddy to Mr. McClellan containing I don't know what & the reply was that he had no desire for office & inclosing [sic] his resignation from three offices - Director in the Mother Church - Trustee of her Estate - & Editor in Chief of the CS Magazines. Frye gave the replies to me & I opened them & gave them to Mrs. Eddy. She dictated a reply accepting his resignation to all but Editor saying she wished him to retain that for the present. I sent the letter to his house by Jno Salchow & he got it on his return from Concord & he called me up by phone acknowledging receipt of letter. Fry [sic] has been ugly all day. Farlow still here.

In the afternoon Mrs. Eddy asked me again if I would serve as her trustee & I said Yes, Mother I will serve in any position where God puts me.

Sept 6 Sunday 6   1908

Trustee   (1)

She told me today that no mortal in this world has
ever suffered as she has.   Miss Peck was sent away today.
A good night last night — nobody called all night long.
Miss Peck told Calvin Frye Mrs Eddy had no consumption.
that this phlegm was from her throat & head. He said
"tell that to Mother" She told it to Mother & Mother thought
she was holding a wrong mental picture & thanked her for
all her good work & sent her home — She left at about 3.30
for Mrs Watsons in Boston.

(2) At about 4.30 Mother called me & said Mr Dickey you promised
me you would be my trustee Will you? I said yes Mother I will
do anything for you. She said Well I want you to a true.
Mrs Sargent urged me to take immediate action & Mrs
Eddy signed a letter to Mr McClellan stating she desired
me to succeed him as Trustee. I afterwards asked Mrs
Sargent if I should let Frye know about this & she said us
Frye came into my room about ½ hour afterwards & I deliberately told him about it I could see he was disturbed
& displeased over it. said he thought it was a great mistake
& he left for his room. It wasn't fin minutes until Mrs.
Sargent called me & told me Mrs Eddy had changed her
mind about the whole thing & when I told her I had told
Frye she reprimanded me & told me Frye manipulated

September   Sunday 6 continued   1908

Mrs Eddy & that I had spoiled the whole thing — told
me she had heard Frye advise Mrs Eddy not to
appoint me Trustee. Later Mrs Eddy told me to get
word to McClellan not to take any action about his re-
segnations. She said Frye told her to do all this except
me's resignation. It looked to me like Frye's manipulation
I am knowing that God is the only power & the only mind
& divine Love governs all.
I was called again & told about getting word to McC.
& again when she had retired to ask me what word I sent
Mr M (seems disturbed)

September 6   Sunday 6   1908

Trustee

She told me today that no mortal in this world has ever suffered as she has. Miss Peck was sent away today. A good night last night - nobody called all night long. Miss Peck told Calvin Frye Mrs. Eddy had no consumption, that this phlegm was <u>from</u> <u>her</u> <u>throat</u> <u>and</u> <u>head</u>. He said "tell that to Mother." She told it to Mother & Mother thought she was holding a wrong mental picture & thanked her for all her good work & sent her home. She left at about 3:30 for Mrs. Watson's in Boston.

At about 4.30 Mother called me and said *Mr. Dickey you promised me you would be my Trustee. Will you?* I said *yes Mother I will do anything for you.* She said *Well I want you to at once Mrs Sargent urged me to take immediate action* & Mrs Eddy signed a letter to McClellan stating she desired me to succeed him as Trustee. I afterwards asked Mrs Sargent if I should let Frye know about this & she said no. Frye came into my room about ½ hour afterwards & I deliberately told him about it I could see he was disturbed & displeased over it. Said he thought it was a great mistake & he left for his room. It wasn't five minutes until Mrs. Sargent called me & told me Mrs. Eddy had changed her mind about the whole thing & when I told her I had told Frye she reprimanded me & told me Frye manipulated Mrs. Eddy & that I had spoiled the whole thing - told me she had heard Frye advise Mrs. Eddy not to appoint me Trustee. Later Mrs. Eddy told me to get word to McClellan not to take any action about his resignation. She said Frye told her to do all this, accept Mc's resignation. It looked to me like Frye's manipulation. I am knowing that God is the only power & this only Mind & divine Love governs all.

I was called again & told about getting word to McC & again when she had retired to ask me what word I sent Mr. M (seems disturbed)

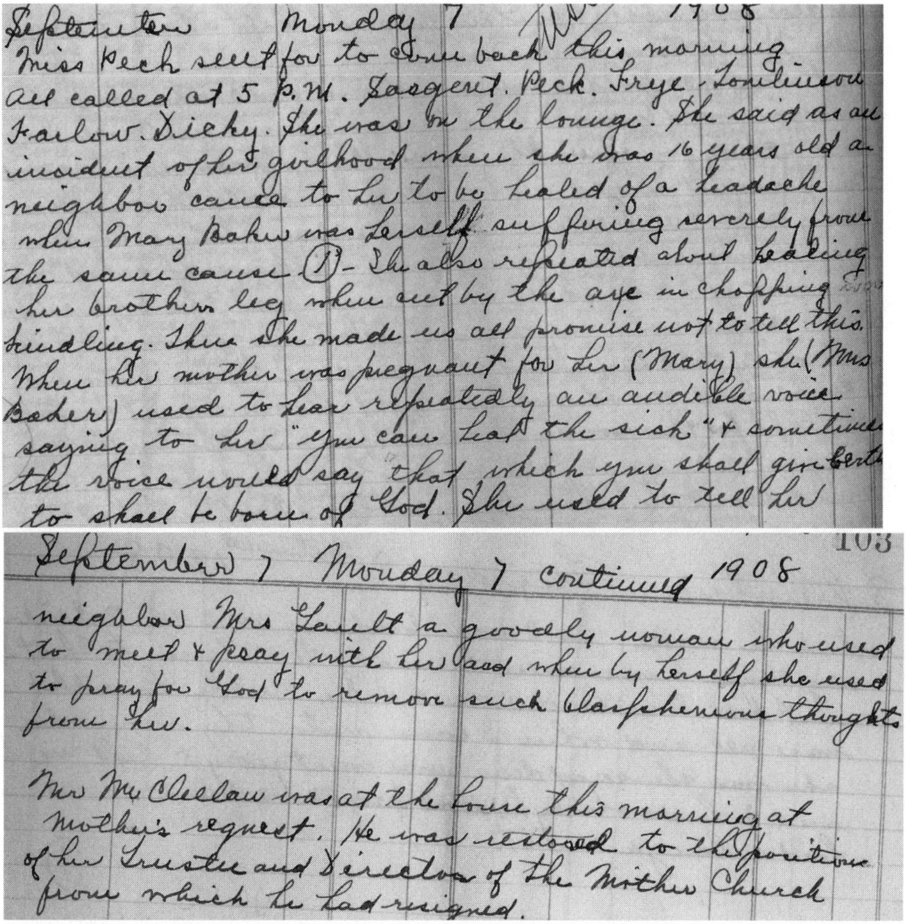

[Handwritten manuscript reproduction appears here]

September   Monday 7   1908

Miss Peck sent for to come back this morning. All called at 5 p.m. Sargent, Peck, Frye, Tomlinson, Farlow, Dickey. She was on the lounge. She said as an incident of her girlhood when she was 16 years old a neighbor came to her to be healed of a headache when Mary Baker was herself suffering severely from the same cause. She also repeated about healing her brother's leg when cut by the axe in chopping kindling. Then she made us all promise not to tell this. When her mother was pregnant for her (Mary) she (Mrs. Baker) used to hear repeatedly an audible voice saying to her, "You can heal the sick" & sometimes the voice would say that which you shall give birth to shall be born of God. She used to tell her neighbor Mrs. Gault a goodly woman who used to meet and pray with her and when by herself she used to pray for God to remove such blasphemous thoughts from her.

Mr McClellan was at the house this morning at Mother's request. He was restored to the position of her Trustee and Director of The Mother Church from which he had resigned.

September 8   Tuesday 8   1908

Miss Peck came back last night and resumed her place in the household, but this time her stay was short; she was told to go again in the forenoon, and after having her trunk packed and all ready to go, she was told she could stay and work out of her claim of materia medica, which seemed to be the belief that caused her to be sent away. (said belief having been encouraged in her through our Leader's asking her so much about material law) After the drive she was again dismissed and told to return to the West and not to remain in Boston.

I asked Mr Frye if I couldn't go to Boston and take back a lot of rings and fobs that had been sent out here for me to select my ring from. He said it looked all right so I left at 2 o'clock. Got as far as the Publishing house, where I met Mr Gaspard the artist who drew Mrs Eddy's picture for Science & Health.

Mr Stewart and I made some suggestions for attesting

September   Tuesday 8 continued, 1908

which he made. As I was looking over the Publishing House I was called hurriedly to return to Chestnut Hill. Our Leader wanted me in the house that was all. and when I came into the room where she was she said dear you went away & left me and I had nobody here but Frye & Tomlinson & we all had a laugh over it.

September 8   Tuesday 8   1908

Miss Peck came back last night and resumed her place in the household, but this time her stay was short; she was told to go again in the forenoon, and after having her trunk packed and ready to go, she was told she could stay and work out of the claims of materia medica, which seemed to be the belief that caused her to be sent away (said belief having been encouraged in her through our Leader's asking her so much about material law). After the drive she was again dismissed and told to return to the West and not remain in Boston.

I asked Mr. Frye if I couldn't go to Boston and take back a lot of rings and fobs that had been sent out here for me to select my ring from. He said it looked all right so I left at 2 o'clock. Got as far as the Publishing house, where I met Mr. Gaspard the artist who drew Mrs. Eddy's picture for Science & Health. Mr. Stewart and I made some suggestions for alterations, which he made. As I was looking over the Publishing House I was called hurriedly to return to Chestnut Hill. Our Leader wanted me in the house that was all and when I came into the room where she was she said *dear you went away & left me & I had nobody here but Frye and Tomlinson &* we all had a laugh on it.

September   Sunday 13   1908

I slipped in at 6.45 to say good night. I said — You have not called upon me to-day for anything, and I feel a little lonesome on account of it. She said well I will call on you now darling to say God bless you to me and I will say God bless you to you. I spoke about how she had given the true knowledge of God to the world even to a greater extent than Jesus had done, and she replied Yes but Jesus had a full knowledge of God, and he gave to the world as much as they could receive. But she said This is the second coming of Christ and it will be the last. Mortals must come into the kingdom through a perfect knowledge of God, and they will each have to do their own work or repeat the experience until the work is done properly. I then said good night and left.

She called me all a little later and said I want to tell you of a strange experience I had years ago. Dr Patterson was sent to the South with a commission to pay sums of money to loyal slave holders. He was captured and confined in a dungeon with only bread and water. Of course this caused me great mental anguish and one night as I lay awake I heard the sound of horses tramping as though a body of soldiery were approaching. I called my maid and said to her do you hear those horses marching, she said no she heard nothing. I asked her to listen, she did so but heard nothing. Well I said I hear them, and as I laid awake pondering, the thought suddenly came to me as clearly as could be. They are moving my husband from one prison to another. The first newspaper we received gave us the news that the prisoners in that prison had been moved. Such experiences came frequently to me, and I tell it to you to show that all the human senses are but beliefs, and again we receive directly the utterances of truth.

I then asked her

September   Sunday 13   1908

I slipped in at 6:45 to say goodnight. I said - you have not called upon me today for anything, and I feel a little lonesome on account of it. She said *well I will call on you now darling to say God bless you to me and I will say God bless you to you.* I spoke about how she had given the true knowledge of God to the world even to a greater extent than Jesus had done, and she replied *Yes, but Jesus had a full knowledge of God, and he gave to the world as much as they could receive. But she said This is the second coming of Christ and it will be the last. Mortals must come into the kingdom through a perfect knowledge of God - and they will each have to do their own work or repeat the experience until the work is done properly.* I then said goodnight and left.

She called us all a little later and said *I want to tell you of a strange experience I had years ago. Dr. Patterson was sent to the South with a commission to pay sums of money to loyal slave holders. He was captured and confined in a dungeon with only bread and water. Of course this caused me great mental anguish and one night as I lay awake I heard the sound of horses tramping as though a body of soldiers were approaching. I called my maid and I said to her do you hear those horses marching, she said no she heard nothing. Well I said I hear them, and as I laid awake pondering, the thought suddenly came to me as clearly as could be. They are moving my husband from one prison to another - the first newspaper we received gave us the news that the prisoners in that prison had been moved. Such experiences came frequently to me, and I tell it to you to show that all the human senses are but beliefs, and again we receive directly the utterances of truth.*

I then spoke up and said "Mother, the wonderful
part of your discovery to me has always been, that you
were enabled to see that what the physical senses
presented to us was only a false belief and not the
real. Oh, she said, wasn't it? Why I can remember
how my father used to think I was possessed, tried
in all sorts of ways to get me to abandon my nonsense
as he called it. The Quakers living in Lynn used
to say to me Why "Mary thee is so well known
and respected thee must not think such things
the people will think thee is dreadful"
        Everything that mortal mind presents
is but the counterfeit of something that is real

        Stewart came out today to consult me
about the picture of Mrs Eddy that was going
into Science & Health. I showed his wife and
friend from Chicago thro the house.

September 14   Monday 14   1908
        note from Adah Still's book

If you knew the sublimity of your hope, the
infinite capacity of your being. the grandeur of
your outlook, you would leave error to destroy
itself. Error has no life. It comes to you
to give it life and you give it temporary
life by admitting it, and so prolong its claim
        to existence

I then spoke up and said Mother, the wonderful part of your discovery has always been that you were enabled to see that what the physical senses presented to us was only a false belief and not the real. *Oh*, she said, *wasn't it? Why I can remember how my father used to think I was possessed, tried to get me in all sorts of ways to abandon my nonsense, as he called it. The Quakers who lived in Lynne [sic] used to say to me "Why Mary thee is so well known and respected thee must not think such things the people will think thee is dreadful."*

Everything that mortal mind presents is but the counterfeit of something that is real.

Stewart came out today to consult me about the picture of Mrs. Eddy that was going into Science & Health. I showed his wife and friend from Chicago thru the house.

September 14   Monday 14   1908
Note from Adah Still's book

If you knew the sublimity of your hope, the infinite capacity of your being, the grandeur of your outlook, you would leave error to destroy itself. Error has no life. It comes to you to give it life and you give it temporary life by admitting it, and so prolong its claim to existence.

October 13   Tuesday 13   1908

A good Lesson   Mrs. Kimball

Mrs. Eddy was fine this morning but after dinner a belief of choking came up & Frye was talking to her after she came in from her drive. He evidently was moralizing to her which didn't help her & she called us all in & said *If one man had another down & was choking him to death & you wanted to help the sufferer which one would you give your attention to?* I said the one who was choking the other - She said *right. Then you wouldn't stand & moralize with the one who was being choked but you would destroy the choker. Well in the same way when disease has a man down & you want to help him you don't begin to tell him a lot of good things & nice sayings - but you destroy the sickness. This is what Jesus did when he found Peter's wife's mother sick of a fever.*

He rebuked the fever & it left her.

Mrs. Kimball got her notice today. Mr. McLellan was sent for tonight & came out to supper & stayed all night - breaking an engagement with his wife & daughter to go to Chickering Hall to hear Mr. Hamlin sing.

October   Wednesday 14   1908

Mrs. Kimball left this morning at 9.30

Mrs. Becker (Jeanette) of Denver arrived this afternoon.

Mr. McClellan went to town this morning & returned this afternoon with his satchel, prepared to stay.

Dickey was given, or obtained, this photo of the Christian Science Publish-
ing Society, formerly the Massachusetts Metaphysical College, which he
shows in at least one entry that he visited. A decade after he served as Mrs.
Eddy's secretary, Adam Dickey, representing the Board of Directors of The
First Church of Christ, Scientist, was to battle the Publishing Society
trustees in the landmark case known later as the Great Litigation. Archibald
McLellan, mentioned in the diary entry on the previous page, was an editor
of publications for the Christian Science movement. He became the fifth
member of the Christian Science Board of Directors and served as chairman
for many years. When Mrs. Eddy wished to move from Pleasant View, it
was McLellan who acquired the Chestmut Hill estate in Newton for her.

October 21 Wednesday 1908

Mrs Eady today received a letter from Stevenson
saying he did not want to leave her & making
complaint about being abused by other members
of the household — Said he had received many
treatments he had not paid for & so had the
horses he drove — Said he could say nothing good
about John Salchow so he would say nothing at
all about him — Mrs Eady had me read the
letter to her so I saw all the contents &
was told to keep the letter which I did. I
also am keeping Jno Salchow's letters. Mrs Eady
told me to tell Stevenson that she had
received the letter & that her attitude was only
one of kindness to him. He asked in his letter
who it was that told him he was going to quit
but she told me to tell him that it was no person

I had quite a long talk with him & tried to
show him the necessity of keeping peace in
the household instead of quarelling with everybody
as he had been doing. He said he would just
like to know who was carrying stories to Mrs
Eady. He also talked a lot about Jno Salchow & threating
to do him up. if he didn't stop what he was doing
ect. ect. He told me a whole lot of trouble about
Jno Salchow. his wife — mother & brother in law

October 21   Wednesday   1908

Mrs. Eddy today received a letter from [Adolph] Stevenson saying he did not want to leave her & making complaint about being abused by other members of the household - Said he had received many treatments he had not paid for & so had the horses he drove - said he could say nothing good about John Salchow so he would say nothing at all about him - Mrs. Eddy had me read the letter to her so I saw all the contents & was told to keep the letter which I did. I also am keeping Jno Salchow's letter. Mrs. Eddy told me to tell Stevenson that she had received the letter & that her attitude was only one of kindness to him. He asked in his letter who it was that told her he was going to quit - but she told me to tell him that it was no person.

I had quite a long talk with him & tried to show him the necessity of keeping peace in the household instead of quarrelling with everybody as he had been doing. He said he would just like to know who was carrying stories to Mrs. Eddy. He also talked a lot about Jno Salchow & threatened to do him up if he didn't stop what he was doing ect ect. He told me a whole lot of trouble about Jno Salchow - his wife - mother and brother in law.

October   Thursday 22   1908

I received a letter from the Board last Tuesday with copies of their letter to Mrs Wilcox of N.C. telling her they had heard she was talking about things that happened in Mrs Eddy's home & Mrs Wilcox's reply saying she was being persecuted because she was a student of Mrs Eddy. The Board wanted to know if I thought Mrs Eddy had taught Mrs Wilcox sufficiently to warrant her in claiming to be Mrs Eddy's student

I replied today saying I wasn't competent to settle that question & that Mrs Eddy herself would settle that if they made inquiry of her

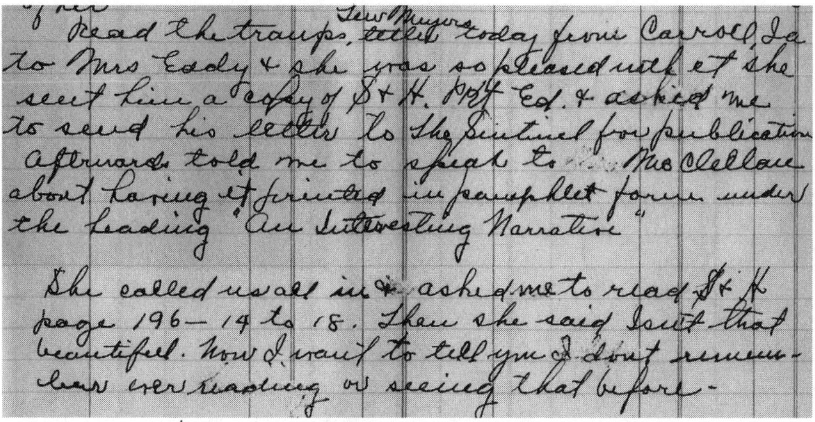

[Handwritten diary entry reproduced in facsimile]

October   Thursday 22   1908

I received a letter from the Board last Tuesday with copies of their letter to Mrs. Wilcox of K.C. telling her that they had heard she was talking about things that happened in Mrs. Eddy's home & Mrs. Wilcox's reply that she was being persecuted because she was a student of Mrs. Eddy. The Board wanted to know if I thought Mrs. Eddy had taught Mrs. Wilcox sufficiently to warrant her in claiming to be Mrs. Eddy's student.

I replied today saying I wasn't competent to settle that question & that Mrs. Eddy herself would settle that if they made inquiry of her.

Read the transps of Lew Meyers letter today from Carroll, Ia to Mrs. Eddy & she was so pleased with it she sent him a copy of S&H. Pvt Ed. & asked me to send his letter to The Sentinel for publication.

Afterwards told me to speak to McClellan about having it printed in pamphlet form under the heading "An Interesting Narrative."

She called us in & asked me to read S&H page 196-14-18. Then she said *Isn't that beautiful? Now I want to tell you I don't remember ever reading or seeing that before.*

December   Wednesday 9   1908

Mrs Stetson of N.Y. arrived today with Mr & Mrs Higgins &
new. York. Sent note to Mrs Eddy by Higgins & Mrs Eddy
replied asking her out at 1 p.m. to take a short drive.
with her. Stetson came at 12.50 I met her in the
parlor. Mrs Eddy had given me instructions to tell
the workers to stay in their rooms during Stetson's
visit. I held her in the parlor & she soon broke into
the subject of McClellan's editorial. She denied
buying the lot. Said they were only considering it,
but had made one payment, said she was pursued
by reporters &c &c. I said nothing.

When Mrs Eddy was in her carriage I brought Mrs
Stetson out & she got in & embraced Mrs Eddy.
When they came back I came out to the carriage
door & helped Stetson out & took her back into the house
& showed her around but she was too preoccupied to
see any thing. I reported to Mrs Eddy & was told
to bring Mrs Stetson up stairs to her room & she
would see her again & for me to stay in the room.
Mrs E. repeated her request to Mrs Stetson to undo
all they had done in N.Y. toward building a branch from
First Church & Stetson promised she would I then took her
down stairs again & Mrs E. sent for her again & I stood
in the elevator entrance & heard her promise Mrs E. again that
she would back out of the deal for the Church property. Asked if
they should return the money subscribed or keep the lot
sell it. Mrs E. said I'll leave that to you.

December   Wednesday 9   1908

Mrs. Stetson of N.Y. arrived today with Mr. & Mrs. Higgins of New York. Sent note to Mrs. E. by Higgins & Mrs. Eddy replied asking her out at 1 p.m. to take a short drive with her. Stetson came at 12.50 I met her in the parlor. Mrs. Eddy had given me instructions to tell the workers to stay in their rooms during Stetson's visit. I held her in the parlor & she soon broke into the subject of McClellan's editorial. She denied buying the lot. Said they were only considering it but had made one payment, said she was pursued by reporters & etc. I said nothing.

When Mrs. Eddy was in her carriage I brought Mrs. Stetson out & she got in & embraced Mrs. Eddy.

When they came back I came out to the carriage door & helped Stetson out & took her back into the house & showed her around but she was too preoccupied to see anything. I reported to Mrs. Eddy & was told to bring Mrs. Stetson upstairs to her room & she would see her again & for me to stay in the room. Mrs. E. repeated the request to Mrs. Stetson to undo all they had done in N.Y. toward building a branch from First Church & Stetson promised she would. I then took her downstairs again and Mrs. E. sent for her again & I stood in the elevator entrance & heard her promise Mrs. E again that she would back out of the deal for the Church property. Asked if they should return the money subscribed or keep the lot & sell it. Mrs. E said *I'll leave that to you.*

December   Wednesday 9   1908

Miss Eveleth told me Miss McDonald had heard a lot of stuff from Stevenson. He repeated to the girls the talk Mrs. E had with Stetson. Talked at table about Mrs. E being lifted into her carriage.

Told English about upholstering auto. Said he was the best man they had ever had in that place that one of Mrs. Eddy's students told him so. (Carpenter) I sent for Miss McDonald & she corroborated all this. Stevenson talks all the time.

Mrs. Eddy loved her carriage rides. She was very interested in her animals and wanted her stable to reflect order and harmony. Stevenson, the driver, caused friction in the household. He is probably the coachman shown in this photo.

December   Monday 14   1908

Mrs. E. talked to me about staying with her but I said I cannot leave my wife. Mrs. E said bring her on here & let her live in Boston & I will pay her expenses – then you can see her frequently. I replied my wife said she would prefer to remain in K.C. with friends than to be here & not be constantly with me.

She afterwards said Mrs. D. was right.

Lillian Dickey had a well furnished room at Chestnut Hill. After Adam Dickey told Mrs. Eddy he needed his wife to be with him, Mrs. Eddy summoned Lillian.

December   Thursday 24   1908

Had a time about Jim Neal[']s letter to McLellan stating that it would be a good idea for Mrs. Eddy to subscribe $1000.00 to the Newton Hospital. I presented it to her but she didn't see it that way.

Told me to write McClellan to say that he should be handed all such matters to look after as he was her business Trustee.

Dec 25   Friday   1908

Mrs. Eddy called me in to her lounge or couch & begged me not to leave her.

Offered to send some body to take care of my wife & pay her expenses. Money was no object. Offered to send for my wife & keep her here if I would only stay. Said she thought if I left her she would not live any longer. Urged me to try & show Mrs. Dickey [...]

it was right for me to stay here three years. Told me I was the best man she ever knew she said. *I never knew anybody who was as good as you are. My husband Dr Eddy & he was next to you. Then my brother Albert Baker approximated you in goodness, but none were so good as you.* Told me I always did every thing right, but that she couldn't depend on Frye - She has made this last statement to me times without number.

January   Monday 11   1909

<u>A good day all around.</u>

Declaring God is all doesn't mean anything if you don't demonstrate it as you go along. Sent love & a kiss to Mrs. Dickey for her goodness & help in allowing me to remain & help her.*

---

* Should we consider these journal entries authentic since only transcriptions remain? Comparison of the dates and events in the Dickey entries with those listed in other diaries and journals of members of the household show exact correlation. It would be unlikely someone could invent so many events with correct dates and times. It's likely the entries are authentic.

Calvin Frye, whom Dickey called in his memoir "a factotum," sits at his desk reading the newspaper in this 1910 photo. He served Mrs. Eddy faithfully from 1882 to 1910, often seeing her through difficult circumstances when others deserted. In 1916 Frye was elected President of The Mother Church.

January   Saturday 30   1909

Again saw necessity of doing own work & talked about it.

Why did St. Paul die? Because he said "I have nothing among you save Jesus Christ and him crucified" instead of him glorifyed.

It appears that household staffers could enjoy the snow in rare moments of recreational time.

February 15	Monday 15	1909

I was talking to Mrs. Eddy today about Luther Burbank & his wonderful work. She said he was only doing things now that have always been possible. She said *Oh how I would like to teach that man Christian Science.* I said what he is doing is certainly scientific. She said *it is Science for <u>All</u> is <u>Mind</u> & material growth is simply mortal mind manifested.*

March   Tuesday 9   1909

Mrs. Hoag was in the room with Mrs. E. all day until 4 o'clock

Mrs. Sargent told me somebody ought to tell McClellan what Ada told me.

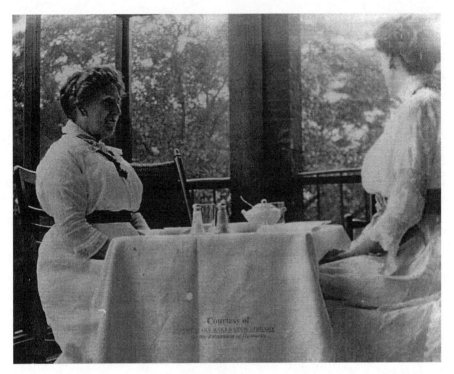

Courtesy of
THE MARY BAKER EDDY LIBRARY
for the Betterment of Humanity

Laura Sargent had been in charge of Mrs. Eddy's household for several years when Mr. Dickey came. Here (r) she is shown with her sister Victoria having luncheon or tea at Chestnut Hill. After Mrs. Eddy's passing, Mrs. Sargent stayed on at Chestnut Hill as caretaker. Courtesy Mary Baker Eddy Collection.

March   Wednesday 10   1909

Then I said. Instead of speaking of joints then I should have said locomotion & action is perfect. She said *yes* Then I said isn't every material conception a counterfeit of the spiritual & shouldn't I declare the perfection of all things? She said *Begin with God not with matter.*

You don't arrive at perfection by thinking of the material organization. Begin with God - Mind & its perfect ideas and keep your thought away from all things material. I said thank you Mother. You have helped me. She said *I love to help you.*

March   Saturday 20   1909

Another faint spell but soon rallied after a little talk in which I took part.

I was given the copyright of her best photograph and asked if I would accept it. I said yes & thanked her. The gift was put in writing. She said *Do you know what that means?* (significantly) I said yes - thanked her.

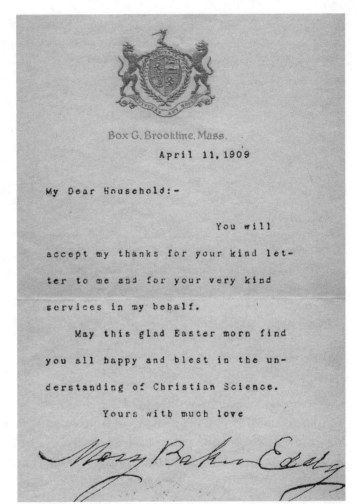

June   Monday 28   1909 Lesson

Now dear you must learn that there is no surplus electricity (lightning) and that we do not suffer from lack of detonations in the atmosphere. God makes the air & atmosphere clear & pure without assistance from any earthly source.

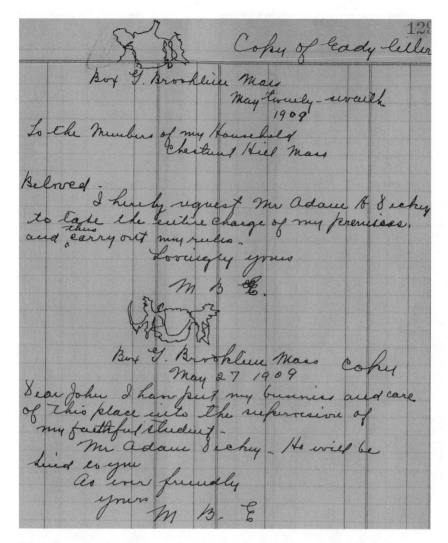

In May of 1909 Mrs. Eddy turned over much of the day-to-day management of Chestnut Hill to Adam Dickey. She continued to be consulted on church and business affiars, and he frequently served as her secretary and advisor in church matters also.

HOW DID DICKEY FINALLY COME TO WRITE A BOOK ABOUT MRS. EDDY?

More than once during Mrs. Eddy's last years she expressed the wish to Dickey that her true story might be told—especially the sacrifices she had endured for the cause of Christian Science. It is clear that she expected him to fulfill this mission.

At some time as he finally began his task of telling about Mrs. Eddy's latter days, Adam Dickey documented the circumstances leading up to the writing of his *Memoirs*, including the pressure not to write it:

The "explanation" document which exists today is a transcribed version evidently done by Lillian Dickey.

Dickey speaks in the document in the following way:

"Adelaid Still & Mrs. Sargent brought me a sealed envelope with the inclosed [sic] [illegible] 'Say in your memoirs that it took thousands to murder Mrs. Eddy' not in the manuscript or printed book. [The Board of Mother Ch has this.]

"When I briefly spoke to the Board of Directors of Mrs. Eddy's wish there was only one member who seemed to feel that I ought to carry out her request. Two of the others were disidedely [sic] opposed to my doing it and did not hesitate to express their opposition. Whatever may be the cause of their opposition I can only guess at, but it seems just as strong at the present day as it was three years ago. I have hesitated to take up the work because of the objections but have always been determined to say my own mind that it should be done, and have felt when the time came I should have no difficulty in proceeding with the work."

Editor's note: Note the differences in the above to the version he gave on page xvi of the *Memoirs* book.

"In a few minues [sic] [after his conversation with Mrs. Eddy, where she asked him to record that she had been mentally murdered] one of the workers and Mrs. Sargent brought me a sealed envelope. In it was a penciled note reiterating the statement she had made in our conversation of a short time before."

The stronger statement, "it took thousands" to mentally murder her was given to the board (above) and wasn't included.

Compare these accounts with the board's suppression explanation in the first, biographical section of this book pp. 108-110.

July   Thursday 1   1909
MBE to AHD

You are the one to take the lead in this house. You will spiritualize your thought & rise to that point won't you dear? Yes! Now I do not want you to think of me personally. When you do you entertain a human sense of me which God will not allow you to perpetuate. When a ship is heavy laden & fighting the seas they lighten the vessel by throwing some of the cargo overboard. Now we are heavy laden & must get rid of materiality in order to get nearer the divine. We must think as God thinks of us & each other.

August   Saturday 14   1909

Today we received word that Edw[ard] A. Kimball passed on last night. I told our Leader about it. She seemed shocked. I told her about him being in belief July 31, 1909.

Sent the following telegram to Mrs. Kimball

Our beloved Leader & members of her household send their loving sympathy to you & yours & pray you may be comforted by the truth which comforts them. The law of the Spirit of life in Christ Jesus makes free from the law of sin & death.

Your loved one is not dead he lives & labors in Truth & Love. A.H.D. Secy.

Dickey's personal likeness of Edward A. Kimball., who has been called the early movement's best lecturer, after Mrs. Eddy.

August	Friday 20	1909

She said to me this morning:

God is preparing a history for you & you are writing it now (meaning that my daily life & experience here is the history).

September	Tuesday 14	1909

All called. Read Luke 22 - *I could talk to you all day on the application of this chapter to this hour, and the fulfillment of its prophecy. Not in desolation but consolation. The work is going on hourly, and means a turning away from the flesh to things of the Spirit.*

September 20   Monday 20   1909

A[u]gusta Stetson's trial begins tomorrow. Mrs. Eddy in speaking of her son told me today that after her boy was born & before the doctor left the house she heard him tell her mother that if she (Mrs Glover) <u>did</u> <u>not</u> nurse her baby she would die and if she <u>did</u> nurse the baby the baby would die. Thereafter no amount of persuasion could induce her to nurse her baby, preferring to die herself.

Lill was with me all afternoon till 7 p.m.

Adam Dickey in his bed at Chestnut Hill. Lillian Dickey could have taken this photograph of Mr. Dickey reading the textbook after she came to live and serve at Chestnut Hill.

October   Wednesday 13   1909

I would take an infant & mentally talk to him & tell him he could not sin, that there was no sin that Love was all. Then as he grew older I would talk to him in the same way & I know the result would be marvelous. I would like to see a child brought up in that way. My child was unruly & I couldn't get him to do a thing I wanted him to, but I didn't know then now I know how to manage a child

George Washington and Andrew Glover, Mrs. Eddy's grandsons, came from South Dakota to visit their grandmother on her 89th birthday. Courtesy Mary Baker Eddy Collection.

Box G, Brookline, Mass.

Oct. 8, 1909

Mr. Adam H. Dickey,

    Beloved

       I hereby caution you to
be careful as my private secretary in
handing letters to me not to task yourself with selecting them but be sure to
give me all the letters that relate to
me and the cause, that are for or against
it and I will take the responsibility of
deciding as to their publication.

Lovingly

Mary Baker Eddy

Mrs. Eddy was glad to hand over daily business decision-making to her secretary, but "being of sound mind" she clearly let him know who remained in charge.

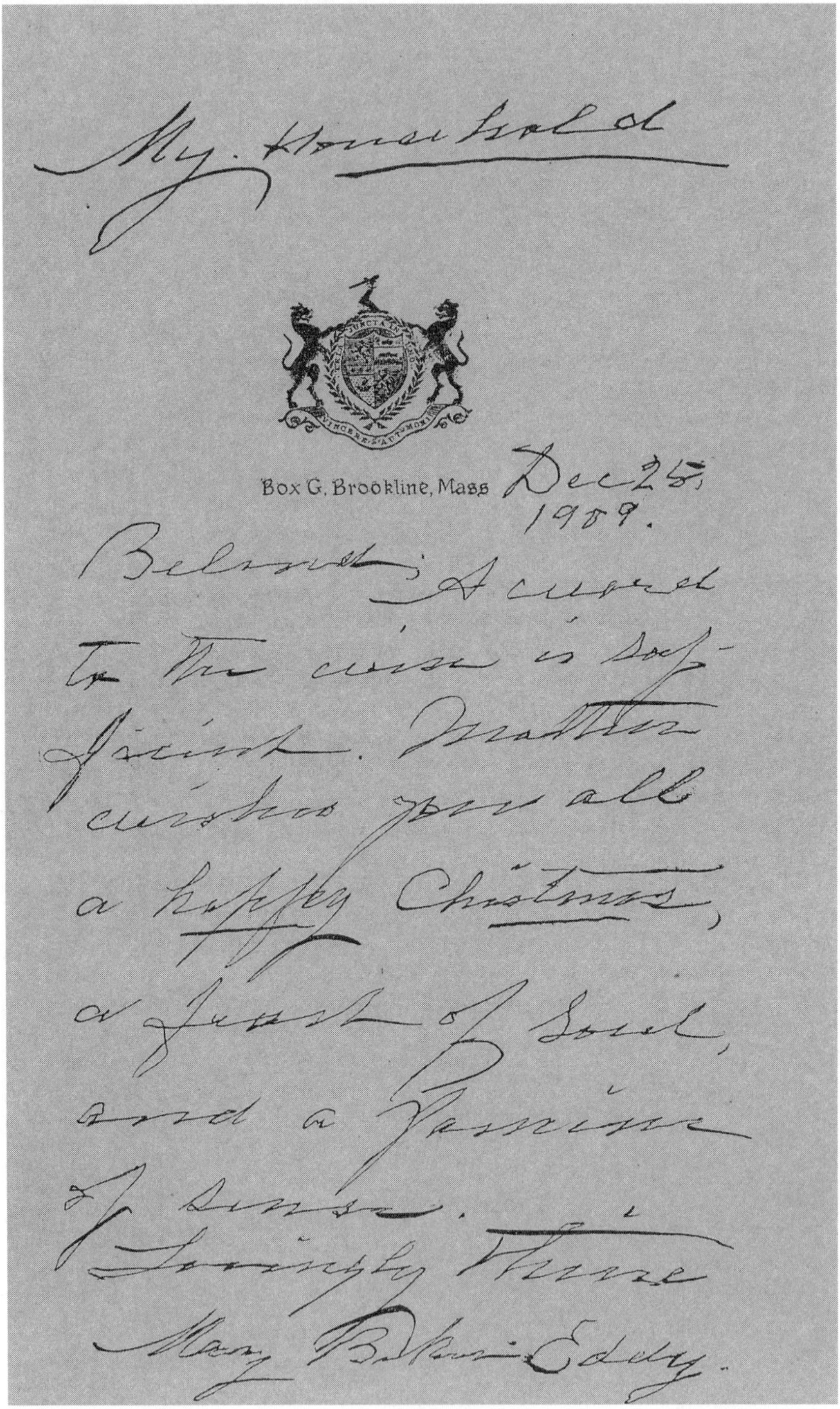

My Household

Box G, Brookline, Mass Dec 25,
1909.

Beloved; A word
to the wise is suf-
ficient. Mother
wishes you all
a happy Christmas,
a feast of Soul,
and a Famine
of sense.
Lovingly thine
Mary Baker Eddy.

Box G, Brookline, Mass.

January 6th, 1910.

Beloved Students:

Your telegram received, with its kind
rehearsal of my permission to allow you
what you have granted me; viz. the presence
and help of so able a student as our beloved
Adam H. Dickey.   You must not take him
from me too often.

God bless you.

Sincerely thine.

Mary Baker Eddy

To Adam H. Dickey's
Students Association.
Kansas City, Mo.

*The leader allowed her secretary to go to Kansas City for his Association meeting. It
was a rare occasion.*

The Leader Passes:

Notes from Lillian Dickey's desk calendar.

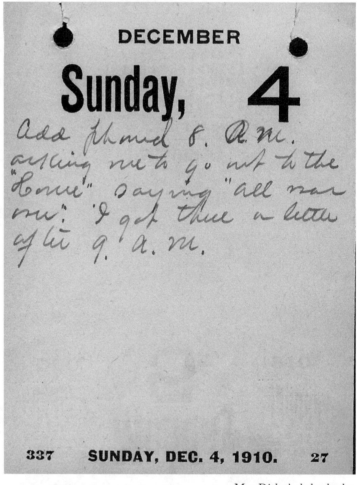

Mrs. Dickey's desk calendar.

Add [Adam] phoned 8 A.M. asking me to go out to the "home" saying all was over. I got there a little after 9 A.M.

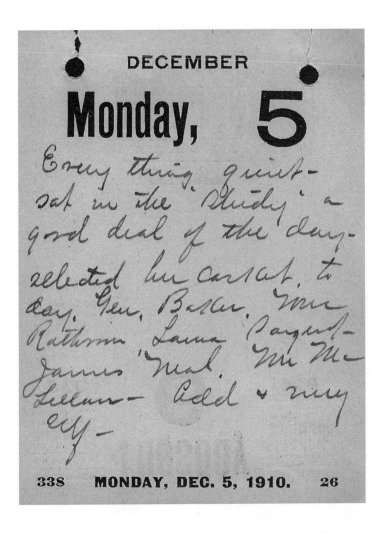

Every thing quiet and sat in the study a good deal of the day. Selected her casket to day, Gen. Baker, Mr. Rathvon, Laura Sargent, James Neal, Mr. McLellan—Add & my self.

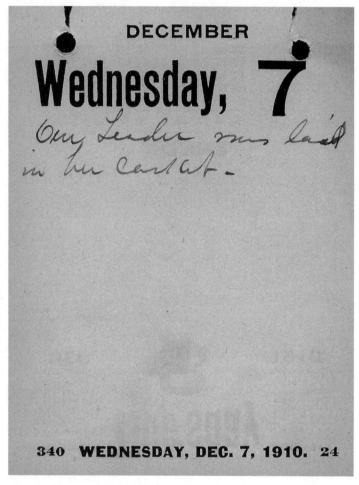

Our Leader was laid in her casket.

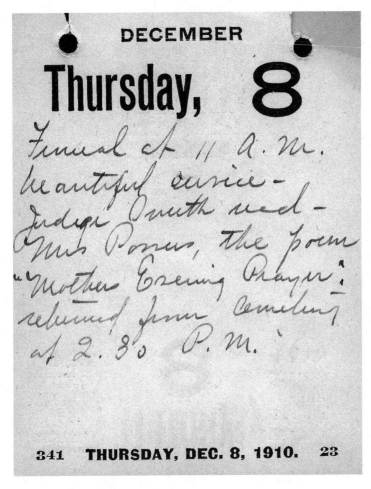

Funeral at 11 a.m.
beautiful service—Judge Smith read— Mrs. Powers, the poem "Moth-
er's Evening Prayer" returned from cemetery at 2.30 P.M.

"Oh, Life that maketh all things new." A peaceful winter snow scene at Chestnut Hill with spring ready to come.

"The wide horizon's grander view."

"The sense of Life that knows no death." A freshly flowing stream beneath the ice near Mary Baker Eddy's home.

Quotations from Samuel Longfellow's poem

Adam Dickey's notes
about his experiences at Chestnut Hill

Keep your watch! Keep your watch!
Jesus said, "Could ye not watch with
me an hour" — "If the good man of the
house had known what hour the thief
would come he would have watched".

in this, you can defeat him in all.
He boasts that he can make a few
for you (for me) six months ahead.
and they work to cover every hour in the night
(~~him & went in~~ & prepared a ~~change in~~ the Watch)

Imposed laws that they can
produce imposing asleep or awake
After a long talk & many illustration
& admonitions we were dismissed.
We were all recalled in a few

moments & asked "now what is (3)
the great necessity I have been
impressing on you — I said
demonstration others said something
else — She said, no! You are all
wrong! you have missed the
~~imprssing of the lesson — & then~~
& called you back to show you, your
ignorance — The lesson is <u>Keep You Watch</u>
dismissed —

Called back again & said what I
have to meet, you will all have to meet
now or again, therefore know them
~~the ... lesson is keep your watch~~

She all solemnly promised to keep our
Watch — Amen,

She said during the course of the talk
"If you will keep your watch I will be a
<u>well woman</u>

If you stay here until you learn how to handle animal magnetism, I will make healers out of you.

I had to do it & did it for 40 years & you must do it. You must rise ~~~ the being in monnesia — or you will have no cause — They tried to overcome me for 40 years, *and I withstood them* & now it has gotten to the point where the students must take up this work & meet animal magnetism ~~~ must do it for yourselves and unless it is done the cause will perish — and we will go another 19000 years with the world sunk into the blackest night. Now will you arouse yourselves you have all the power of God with

Typed summary notes included with the Collection

MRS. EDDY

    Moved to Concord   MEMO. II -1

    Consenting to have a record
    made of her voice   Notes 1 e

    Never rejected anything
    that had any good in it
                Notes 1 f

    While Mr. D. was in Mrs.
    Eddy's home there were
    20 or 30 persons who came
    and went because they did
    not measure up to the re-
    quirements   Notes 1 h

    Her great love for mankind
                Notes 3 b

MRS. EDDY   Diary
   "Science and Senses"   107 #1
      (Her determination

                             Diary
   Scolding Students   111
                 Notes   1-i
                 "   4 d-e

   Ordered carriage shortly before
passing on showing she had no thot
of death.   NOTES 18 b

Her Passing on
   Undertaker's statement regarding
   Mrs. Eddy's condition.

Her high thot of service Notes 6 a- b -

Interested in Flying machines " 6 f

Her pictureh her room   " 6a- 11

Asked Mr. D. about the furniture
in her room   "   18 a

MRS. EDDY

Her great love and appreciation
of the work of Jesus   14 a

MRS. EDDY

CARRYING HER TO BED   Diary
                                                   196

Her human will   199

Continuance to lecture
on C. S. even tho stones
and bricks were thrown thru
windows. (Determination)   NOTES 15
Continuance to write articles
on slavery when she was in the
South in spite of her husband's
protests. (Determination)   NOTES 17 a

Susceptibility to human thot
                                      257 #2

Speaking of her wonderful discovery
she said, "Wasn't it wonderful !"
                                      257 #3
                             NOTES 9 d

```
      TEACHING  .
Diary    182    Sufferer closer to God
         190    Meeting hypnotism for the world
         195    We are not in matter: we are spirit
         253    After death
         257    #1. Second coming of Christ

Notes 4 a,     Her requestfor students to work
        b, c   audibly that she might know how
               they were working


  "     5      Tomlinson - old age


  "     6 e    Told Mr. D. never to say that
               she could never have a return
               of an old belief.


  "     8 a    Told Mr. D. never to refer to
               a wrong idea.


  "     8 b    C. S. mentalizing the universe etc


  "    13 a    How good can flow from departed
               to those on this plain of thot.
               Limitation mortal mind puts on
               itself prevents us from convers-
               ing with those who have passed on.
```

MRS. EDDY

Of her purchasing a lot
in Mt. Auburn Cemetery and
countermanding the order the
next day   <u>NOTES</u> 6a - 1

Her bedroom Furnishings "   6a - 2

Occasion when she showed herself to newspaper reporters
and her picture was taken
              <u>NOTES</u> 6a - 3

Her experience with an
automobile.   "   6a - 4

The quickness with which
she got mental impressions
from others. Re. telescope
            <u>NOTES</u> 6a - 6

Her fondness for children
and the little baby that
visited her.   <u>NOTES</u> 6a - 7

Her aversion to Electricity
           <u>NOTES</u>   7

Asked Mr. D. "Did you ever
t ake such a long step that
you fell down   <u>NOTES</u>   9 c